Remember Your Joy

A Bible Study of Salvation Stories in the Old Testament

Courtney Doctor
& Melissa Kruger

Table of Contents

Eve's Offspring

Salvation Is Promised

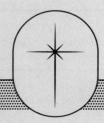

Courtney Doctor

Introduction

As a child, I desperately wanted to wear glasses. But no matter how many times I faked my eye exams, I never got them. Be careful what you wish for! After my last few birthdays, it seems I don't need to fake bad eyesight anymore. My vision has become quite blurry unless I can get a little distance from what I'm trying to see. My optometrist decided it was time for me to start using reading glasses. These were not exactly the glasses I dreamt of as a child.

I now own close to ten pairs of "readers." They're scattered throughout my house—by my kitchen sink, on my desk, by my favorite armchair, next to my bathroom sink, two in my purse, one in my car—because I never know when I might need them. With them, even the blurry little words on the back of a shampoo bottle become clear. The fine print at the bottom of a page is legible. With the readers, I'm able to differentiate between a "6" and an "8."

Seeing through this new lens allows me to see more clearly.

In a similar way, reading Scripture through the lens of biblical theology—as one cohesive story—helps us see more clearly God's magnificent plan of redemption. The Bible doesn't comprise individual stories, unrelated and disjointed from each other. We aren't meant to study Noah, Abraham, Moses, and David simply to glean a moral lesson from their lives.

The Bible is more than a collection of short stories; it's one unified story from beginning to end. It's an epic story of God winning the greatest war that has ever occurred. Each of the characters we meet is a part of this epic battle. They're not the heroes of their individual stories; they point us to the one, true hero of our souls.

This great war began long ago in a garden with a lie, a rebellion, a curse, and a promise.

In the beginning, God made a beautiful world full of good things. He placed Adam and Eve in a garden and enjoyed unbroken fellowship with them. Everything was very good. But this goodness did not go untested. The serpent, the father of all lies, tempted Adam and Eve to distrust and disobey God's Word. He spread false doubt about God's goodness and spurred them on in their rebellion. When they chose to follow the lies of Satan over the truth of God, they drew a battle line and sided with God's enemy.

For all practical purposes, the story should have ended right there. The headline should have read, "God's Foolish Children Abandon Him and Die." But it didn't end there. It took a glorious turn because God loves his children and will stop at nothing to save them.

God stepped into this scene of treason and rebellion, and spoke first to the serpent—the deceiver, the enemy—with both a curse and a promise.

I will put enmity between you [serpent] and the woman, and between your offspring and her offspring; he shall bruise your head, and you shall bruise his heel. (Gen. 3:15)

The Evil One thought he had made allies of Adam and Eve. But God switched the narrative, redefined the battle lines, and proclaimed instead that there would be enmity between the serpent and the woman, and between their respective offspring. God promised to do battle—not *with* Adam and Eve but *for* them. The promise was that her offspring would do what Adam should have done: he would crush the head of the serpent.

As we turn the pages of the Old Testament, we should consider each new person we're introduced to, asking, "Is this the One? Is this the Promised One who will defeat the Evil One? Is this the seed, born of a woman, who will crush the head of the serpent?" Each person we encounter is not the hero of an unrelated story with a moral message to impart—each person is a thread woven into the great tapestry waiting to unveil the true hero. He is the One who accomplishes our salvation by doing exactly what God promised Adam and Eve.

In this study, we will trace the promised seed of the woman, looking at Old Testament accounts that give us a glimpse, a foreshadowing, of the greater salvation Jesus wins: Noah and the ark, Abraham and Isaac, Moses and the Israelites in the desert, Rahab and the spies, David and Goliath, and David and Mephibosheth. In each encounter, we'll see how God faithfully fulfilled his promise as he prepared us for the ultimate offspring who brought us eternal salvation.

Each story will be accompanied by a symbol that represents an aspect of our salvation. These symbols are intended to be visual reminders that help instruct, remind, and cause us to have deep joy in the reality of our salvation. David once wrote, "Restore to me the joy of your salvation" (Ps. 51:12). Our hope is that the joy of your salvation—and your praise of the One who accomplished it—will increase as you see afresh the victory he won on your behalf.

What to Expect

DAY 1 **Observation**	Day 1 will always be observation—reading the passage and asking the question: *What does the text say?* In this study, we will primarily be reading Old Testament narratives. Day 1 will involve slowly reading the passage several times while paying attention to details like characters, setting, and plot. You may have questions as you read. It's OK to not have all the answers or to be confused as you read certain passages. Write your questions in the margins and see if you can answer them by the end of the week.
DAY 2 **Interpretation**	Day 2 will focus on interpretation. We'll read the passage again and ask: *What does it mean?* We'll focus on details like the author, original audience, and context of the passage as we begin to interpret it.
DAY 3 **Interpretation**	Day 3 will continue to concentrate on interpretation by asking: *What does the New Testament say?* We'll read other relevant and related passages in Scripture and ask the question: *How does the rest of Scripture help me understand this text?*
DAY 4 **Application**	Day 4 will focus on application. We'll ask the question: *How does this text transform me?* As we pay attention to what this passage teaches us about God and ourselves, we'll consider what God has done and what we are to do in response. God's Word transforms how we think, what we love, and what we do. Time with Jesus changes us from the inside out.
DAY 5 **Reflection**	Each week will end on Day 5 with a reflection. After reading the reflection, you'll have an opportunity to summarize what you've learned that week.

Please plan on approximately 20 minutes of study each day (or 1.5 hours each week). Each day will begin with prayer—a time for you to ask God to meet you as you study his living and active Word. We recommend you have a print Bible in front of you, rather than using an app on your phone or computer. You'll need it for cross-referencing verses, and it helps you more readily see the passage in its context. The provided Bible passages are from the English Standard Version, but feel free to use whatever translation you prefer.

MEMORY WORK

A memory verse(s) is provided each week. Spend a few minutes each day working on memorizing it. The discipline of hiding God's Word in your heart will bear much fruit in your own life and the lives of those around you.

DISCUSSION QUESTIONS

At the end of each chapter, you'll find a list of discussion questions. These are based on the work you've done throughout the week. We've also included an "icebreaker" question and a "warm-up" question. Both are intended to be a quick, easy, and fun way to get the group going. Keep the answers to these short so you have plenty of time to dig into the text together.

VIDEOS

We hope to be able to provide videos of the keynote teaching sessions from TGCW22. Each video will align with the chapters and, Lord willing, be available after the conference in June 2022 at https://www.thegospelcoalition.org/conference/tgcw22.

May the Lord richly bless you with the presence of his Spirit, insight into his Word, more love for his Son, and renewed joy in his great salvation!

"May those who love your salvation say continually, 'Great is the LORD!'"

Psalm 40:16

Noah and the Ark

Salvation Is Needed

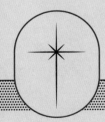

Melissa Kruger

INTRODUCTION

This week, we'll be reading a story that's probably familiar to most of us: Noah's ark. It's been colorfully portrayed in movies, storybooks, and children's nursery décor for generations. As we delve into these chapters, I hope you'll glean fresh insights—both about God's righteousness and our profound need of salvation. Sometimes a story can be so familiar to us that we miss its most important message.

As you read, reflect upon this salvation story in light of the promise in Genesis 3:15: "I will put enmity between you and the woman, and between your offspring and her offspring; he shall bruise your head, and you shall bruise his heel." Consider the ways God was keeping his promise to Adam and Eve as he worked salvation for Noah and his family.

MEMORY VERSE

"But Noah found favor in the eyes of the LORD."

Genesis 6:8

PRAYER FOR THE WEEK

Lord, guide me as I read your Word. Let me learn from the story of Noah's ark new insights about the greatness of your salvation. Give me wisdom as I read, and help me see wonderful things in your Word. Speak to me, teach me, and show me how to live. Soften my heart and bring conviction where it is needed. Lead me in paths of righteousness that I may glorify you in all things. Restore to me the joy of your salvation and renew a right spirit within me.

In Jesus's name I pray. Amen.

What Does the Text Say?

Today we're going to spend our time simply observing the text. Good observation begins with listening to the story and absorbing all the details. Begin your time with prayer, and then read the text carefully. If possible, read it out loud.

READ GENESIS 6:5–8:19

1. Go back through the text and observe:

    a. Who are the characters in this story?

    b. What happens in the story? Briefly summarize the story in your own words.

    c. Who is saved in this story, and by what means?

2. List everything you learn about Noah.

3. Why was Noah instructed to build an ark (Gen. 6:13)?

4. How was the ark to be built (Gen. 6:14–16)? What items were to go inside the ark (Gen. 6:17–22)?

5. Fill out the chart below to help with a timeline of the flood. How long were Noah and his family on the ark?

Verses	What happened?	On what month and/or day did it happen?
Gen. 7:11–12	All the fountains of the deep burst forth, and it rained	Second month, 17th day
Gen. 7:17		
Gen. 8:2–4		
Gen. 8:13		
Gen. 8:14–19		

6. What did the flood do to the earth? To animals? To people?

7. Did any details in the story surprise or confuse you? Do you have any questions about the passage?

What Does the Text Mean?

Today we'll spend our time diving deeper into our understanding of the text as we seek to interpret what it means. Good interpretation flows from thoughtful observation, so take the time to read the passage again today. Begin your time with prayer, asking God to give you wisdom as you study.

READ GENESIS 6:5–8:19

1. What do you learn about God from this passage (hint: pay attention to every time God speaks)?

2. What do you learn about mankind? How do Genesis 6:5 and 6:11–13 support Paul's assertion in Romans 3:9–18?

3. Read Genesis 6:7–8. The Hebrew word chen can be interpreted as "favor" or "grace" in English. Commentator James Dixon translates this verse: "But Noah found grace in the eyes of the Lord."[1] As you consider what you read in Romans 3 about the sinfulness of man, what does it mean that Noah found grace or favor in the eyes of the Lord?

4. God's grace to us bears fruit (see Gal. 5:22) in our lives. Read Genesis 6:9, 22, and 7:5. What fruit do you see in Noah's life as a result of God's grace?

Numerous faithful followers of God are called "righteous" in Scripture. It doesn't mean that Noah was sinless or perfect, but that his life was marked by following God. New Testament scholar (and my husband) Michael Kruger explains this category of a "righteous man":

> Noah is described this way in Genesis 6:9: "Noah was a righteous man, blameless in his generation. Noah walked with God." Joseph of Arimathea was described this way in Luke 23:50: "Now there was a man named Joseph, from the Jewish town of Arimathea. He was a member of the council, a good and righteous man." Zechariah and Elizabeth were described this way: "And they were both righteous before God, walking blamelessly in all the commandments and statutes of the Lord" (Luke 1:6). And there are countless passages throughout Scripture that contrast the "righteous" with the "wicked" (Ps. 1:5–6; 32:1–2; 37:16–17; 75:10).
>
> So, what exactly is a "righteous" person? Surely, we cannot suggest that all these passages are simply referring to the imputed righteousness of Christ (as important as that is). No, it appears the Bible uses this category of the "righteous man" for believers who display a marked consistency and faithfulness in walking with God. Of course, this doesn't mean these people are perfect, sinless, or able to merit their own salvation. It simply means that the Spirit is at work in such a way that they bear steady fruit in their lives.[2]

---

[1] James Dixon, Genesis Expository Thoughts (Webster: Evangelical Press, 2005), 160.
[2] Michael Kruger, "Is Anyone More Holy Than Anyone Else?" Canon Fodder, accessed March 8, 2021. https://www.michaeljkruger.com/is-anyone-more-holy-than-anyone-else-the-missing-category-of-the-righteous-man/

5. Think of this story in light of the promise in Genesis 3:15. How was God keeping his promise through his work in Noah's life?

6. Consider Genesis 7:11–24.

   a. Whom does God save? How does he save them?

   b. Whom does God judge? How does he judge them?

   c. In what ways do we see both God's mercy and justice in this passage?

What Does the New Testament Say?

As we read Old Testament stories, it's helpful to make New Testament connections. Today, we'll look at references in the New Testament that mention or highlight this story from the Old Testament. Open your time in prayer, asking for wisdom to read and understand this story in light of the bigger story of Scripture.

1. Read Matthew 24:36–44. How were the people unprepared in the days of Noah? In what ways do you think Jesus's second coming might be similar?

2. Read 1 Peter 3:18–22. What does Peter compare the flood to in this passage? How does Noah's ark symbolize Christ's salvation for us?

3. Read 2 Peter 2:4–10. How does Peter appeal to Noah's ark as a warning for us today?

4. Read 2 Peter 3:1–7.

    a. In what ways are Peter's words comparable to Jesus's words in Matthew 24:36–44?

b. How will Jesus's second coming be similar to the flood?

c. How will it be different?

5. Why is it significant that the ark only had one door and that the Lord shut them in (see Gen. 6:16 and 7:16)? How is this similar to Jesus's second coming (see Acts 4:12)?

6. Hebrews 11:6–7 tells us, "And without faith it is impossible to please him, for whoever would draw near to God must believe that he exists and that he rewards those who seek him. By faith Noah, being warned by God concerning events as yet unseen, in reverent fear constructed an ark for the saving of his household. By this he condemned the world and became an heir of the righteousness that comes by faith." What do you learn about Noah from this passage? How did Noah please God?

7. How do these New Testament passages help you better understand the story of Noah as foreshadowing our salvation in Jesus? In what ways is this story relevant for us today?

How Does the Text Transform Me?

We've observed the text and interpreted its meaning. Now it's time to take what we've studied and apply it to our lives. Pray for the Spirit to transform you as you study God's Word today.

READ GENESIS 6:5–8:19

1. As you consider this story, how does it help you better understand your salvation in Christ? Why do you need to be saved?

2. Noah's faith in God led to his obedience to God. In what ways does your faith need to be accompanied by obedience to God's Word? Is there disobedience that you need to confess, repent of, and ask forgiveness for? Take the time to prayerfully reflect this morning on how your faith could overflow into a deeper walk with Jesus.

3. In this story, we can observe so clearly both God's salvation and also his judgment of sin. In what ways does this story affect your view of God? How is God's judgment of sin both comforting and uncomfortable at the same time?

4. Yesterday, we read from 2 Peter 2:9–10: "the Lord knows how to rescue the godly from trials, and to keep the unrighteous under punishment until the day of judgment, and especially those who indulge in the lust of defiling passion and despise authority." What gives you hope in this passage? What do you learn from the warnings in this passage?

5. 2 Peter 3:7 warns: "But by the same word the heavens and earth that now exist are stored up for fire, being kept until the day of judgment and destruction of the ungodly."

   a. Why is evangelism so important? Why is it an essential part of loving your neighbor?

   b. Is there someone in your life who needs salvation? What steps can you take this week to share with them the good news about Jesus?

6. Noah and his family witnessed terrible destruction all around them as the floods overcame the earth. They must have been so thankful to be safe inside the ark. Ultimately, their salvation was only temporary. All of the people on the ark eventually died. How is our salvation in Jesus a greater salvation? Why should it give us greater joy?

7. How does the story of Noah's ark encourage you to believe, live, or love differently as a result of your study this week?

When we lived overseas in Scotland, a friend sent our newborn daughter a beautiful, pastel-colored quilt with playful images detailing various animals boarding the ark. Since we were living in a one-bedroom flat, I hung the quilt beside the crib in an attempt to create a small space that felt like a nursery within our bedroom. Others sent us colorful books and rhyming songs all about Noah and his ark. These peaceful images surrounded my new baby daughter.

As I read and reread these chapters in Genesis this week, I kept thinking about how these idyllic childhood images differ from the biblical account. The reality of the flood must have been more like a horror film than a nursery rhyme (and probably not something that anyone who lived through would have put on a quilt for a baby). It was a scene of utter devastation—earth, animals, and people all destroyed by torrential waters.

Even more unsettling, this flood didn't occur as the result of climate change or some uncommon weather pattern. It happened by the very hand of God because the wickedness of man was so great upon the earth. God's holiness met with his righteousness in a terrifying display of judgment.

While we can easily sing of and rejoice in the mercy and grace of God, it's uncomfortable for many of us to even acknowledge God's judgment. However, God is so perfectly good that he hates all forms of evil. His holiness cannot coexist with wickedness. We may not want to, but we need to ponder the judgment of God. As author and pastor J. I. Packer notes:

> One of the most striking things about the Bible is the vigor with which both Testaments emphasize the reality and terror of God's wrath. "A study of the concordance will show that there

are more references in Scripture to the anger, fury, and wrath of God, than there are to His love and tenderness" (A. W. Pink, The Attributes of God, p. 75).[1]

Yes, the flood account is a picture of salvation for Noah, but it's also a terrifying display of God's displeasure. It's not a fly-off-the-handle-in-a-fit-of-rage type of destruction. It's a righteous and just judgment that God patiently restrained for more than 100 years while he prepared a mode of salvation for Noah.

Why was Noah saved from this righteous judgment that befell everyone around him? Hebrews tells us: "by faith" (Heb. 11:7). Yes, his faith overflowed into obedience, but Noah was saved by faith in the promised offspring (Gen. 3:15) who was fully revealed in the person of Jesus. Just as there was only one ark to save Noah from the flood, there is only one person by whom any of us can be saved and live a new life: Jesus. Noah's temporary salvation came by the ark; his eternal salvation came by Jesus.

The message of the gospel actually begins with the bad news: the righteous judgment of God is coming. God will destroy the earth again and this time by fire (2 Pet. 3:7). It will come when we least expect it. How can we escape? Who is our ark of salvation?

Only Jesus can save us! He gives us his perfect righteousness so that we can welcome the day of the Lord, rather than cower in fear. Hear this good news from Romans 5:6–11:

> For while we were still weak, at the right time Christ died for the ungodly. For one will scarcely die for a righteous person— though perhaps for a good person one would dare even to die— but God shows his love for us in that while we were still sinners, Christ died for us. Since, therefore, we have now been justified by his blood, much more shall we be saved by him from the wrath of God. For if while we were enemies we were reconciled to God by the death of his Son, much more, now that we are reconciled, shall we be saved by his life. More than that, we also

---

[1] J. I. Packer, Knowing God (Downers Grove: Intervarsity Press, 1973), 134–135.

rejoice in God through our Lord Jesus Christ, through whom we have now received reconciliation.

All who believe in Christ are saved from the coming wrath of God. This salvation is the reason the gospel is such good news—in Jesus we have an ark of righteousness to save us from the coming destruction. No matter what happens to us in this life, no matter what sufferings we endure, we can rejoice in God's gift of salvation and the hope of eternal life in Christ.

As we begin this study on salvation stories, let me encourage you to make sure you are in the faith. Believe in Jesus, the ark of your salvation. If you are unsure about your faith, talk to a trusted Christian in your life. Pray this prayer today:

Jesus, I believe you are the Son of God, and I want to know you more. Make me your child and teach me your ways. Save me by your grace. Amen.

If you are a Christian, consider these questions today:

1. As you consider this story, how does it help you better understand your salvation in Christ? Why do you need to be saved?

2. Noah's faith in God led to his obedience to God. In what ways does your faith need to be accompanied by obedience to God's Word? Is there disobedience that you need to confess, repent of, and ask forgiveness for? Take the time to prayerfully reflect this morning on how your faith could overflow into a deeper walk with Jesus.

Icebreaker Question

If you were on Noah's ark, what animal would you most want to share a room with?

Warm-Up Question

Can you share a time when you rightly got a punishment you deserved (e.g., getting a speeding ticket, being grounded in high school, paying for something you broke, etc.)?

READ GENESIS 6:5–22

1. Why did God bring the flood? Why did he save Noah? (Consider why he saved Noah in light of Genesis 3:15 and Hebrews 11:6–7.)

2. How does this story help you better understand your salvation in Christ? Why do we need salvation?

3. In this story, we can observe so clearly both God's salvation and his judgment of sin. How does this story impact your view of God? How is God's judgment of sin both comforting and uncomfortable at the same time?

4. 2 Peter 3:7 warns: "But by the same word the heavens and earth that now exist are stored up for fire, being kept until the day of judgment and destruction of the ungodly."

   a. Why is evangelism so important? Why is it an essential part of loving your neighbor?

   b. What are your greatest obstacles to sharing the gospel with others?

   c. Who in your life can you share the good news of Jesus with?

5. Read Matthew 24:36–44. How does the story of Noah provide insight about how we should live today?

6. Noah's faith in God led to his obedience to God (he built an ark in the middle of dry land). How have you experienced the blessing of obeying God, even when it didn't make sense to others?

7. Share with your group one thing you learned about God this week or one way you hope to change.

8. Share with your group how this salvation story reminds you of the joy of your salvation in Christ.

Ram in the Thicket

Salvation Is Substitutionary

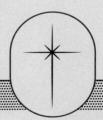

Courtney Doctor

INTRODUCTION

Last week we left Noah, his family, and all the animals exiting the ark onto dry ground. If we'd kept reading, we would have read that God spoke to Noah and gave him the same instructions he originally gave to Adam and Eve: "be fruitful and multiply," and fill the earth (Gen. 9:7). Noah obeyed and Genesis 10–11 chronicles his descendants. At the end of chapter 11, we're introduced to one of Noah's great, great, great grandsons . . . Abram. We'll turn our attention to him this week, but, because we are tracing the seed of Adam and Eve, it's important to note that Abram (soon to be renamed Abraham) descended from Noah, who descended from Adam and Eve.

With Abraham, we find one of the most challenging stories in all of Scripture: the sacrifice of his son, Isaac. As you read, you might wonder how God could have asked such a thing, how Abraham could have proceeded with such a thing, or how Isaac could have agreed to such a thing. Our questions only intensify when we remember that we are tracing the promised seed. What will happen to the promise if Isaac dies?

As we see the whole story play out, I hope you will see Abraham's deep trust and radical faith. But, even more importantly, I hope you will marvel at God's provision for Abraham, Isaac—and us.

MEMORY VERSE

"And Abraham lifted up his eyes and looked, and behold, behind him was a ram, caught in a thicket by his horns. And Abraham went and took the ram and offered it up as a burnt offering instead of his son. So Abraham called the name of that place, 'The LORD will provide': as it is said to this day, 'On the mount of the LORD it shall be provided.'"

Genesis 22:13-14

PRAYER FOR THE WEEK

Father, thank you for your living Word. Please open my eyes so I can see the beauty of who you are. Show me how great your love is for me—so great that you provided your only Son to be sacrificed for me. Help me to respond in true worship, deep trust, and radical obedience.

In Jesus's name I pray. Amen.

What Does the Text Say?

Today we're going to spend time observing the text as we consider what it says. Begin your time with prayer, and then read the text carefully. If possible, read it out loud.

READ GENESIS 22:1–19

1. Go back through the text and observe:

    a. Who are the characters in this story? How are they described?

    b. What happens in this story? Retell it in your own words.

    c. Who is saved in this story, and by what means are they saved?

2. What geographical places are mentioned?

3. What three phrases are used to describe Isaac's relationship with Abraham (v. 2)?

4. How many times in this passage does God say, "your son, your only son"?

5. What, if anything, do you find unusual about verse 5?

6. Who carried the wood up the mountain (v. 6)?

7. Reread verse 14. What was "that place" (v. 2), and what will the Lord do in that place?

8. What/who was supposed to die? What/who died instead?

9. Did any details in the story surprise or confuse you? Do you have any questions about the passage?

What Does the Text Mean?

Today we'll shift from just observing the text and begin asking questions like, *What does it mean?* Good interpretation flows from thoughtful observation, so take the time to read the passage again today. Start your time with prayer, asking God to give you wisdom and insight as you study.

READ GENESIS 22:1–19

1. What do you think it means that "God tested Abraham" (v. 1)?

2. What do you learn about Abraham and Isaac's obedience in verses 3, 9, and 10? Use three to five words to describe their obedience.

3. What is revealed in Abraham's words to the servants: "Stay here with the donkey; I and the boy will go over there and worship and come again to you" (v. 5)?

4. In 2 Chronicles 3:1 we read, "Then Solomon began to build the house of the LORD in Jerusalem on Mount Moriah." What significance do you see in the fact that the temple was built in the same location that God asked Abraham to sacrifice Isaac? In what ways is verse 14 a foreshadowing of Christ?

5. In verses 17–18, three things are said of Abraham's promised offspring. What do you think each of them might mean?

In Genesis 12, 15, and 17 we read that God made covenantal promises to Abraham. God promised that Abraham would be the father of a great nation (Gen. 12:2), that his offspring would be as numerous as the stars in the sky (Gen. 15:5), and that kings and nations would come from him (Gen. 17:6). If Isaac had died, all of those promises would have died with him.

6. In what way do you see "the seed" promised in Genesis 3:15 being preserved here?

What Does the New Testament Say?

Augustine, an early church father from Africa, famously said about the Old and New Testaments, "The new is in the old concealed; the old is in the new revealed." Others have said, "The new is in the old contained; the old is in the new explained." They all mean that in the Old Testament, we see shadows of what is to come; in the New Testament, those shadows become substance. So, on day three of each week, we are going to turn to the New Testament in order to see how God reveals and explains the fullness of what he did in the Old Testament.

1. In Luke 3:22, what did the Father call Jesus?

2. Read John 1:29–36. What did John the Baptist call Jesus twice?.

3. John 3:16 says, "For God so loved the world, that he gave his only Son, that whoever believes in him should not perish but have eternal life."

   a. In what way did God do the exact thing he spared Abraham from doing?

b. What did Jesus do that Isaac didn't?

c. Reread Genesis 22:7–8. What question did Isaac ask, and how did Abraham answer?

d. According to John 3:16, how did God ultimately answer?

4. Read John 19:17–18. Thinking about everything you've studied so far this week, what similarities and what differences do you see between Isaac and Jesus?

5. Read Romans 8:31–32. God spared both Isaac and Abraham in Genesis 22, but he did not spare himself or his only beloved Son. As a result, what does Paul say we can know about how God relates to us?

The story of Abraham begins in Genesis 12 with God calling a 75-year-old Abraham to leave his home, family, and country and follow him. Abraham obeyed. God promised Abraham that he would give land to Abraham's offspring/seed. The problem was Abraham had no children. Yet.

God came to Abraham a second and third time and promised him not just an offspring, but offspring as numerous as the stars in the sky—and Abraham believed God (Gen. 15:5–6).

Abraham waited and waited for the child of promise, the offspring of faith, to be born. Isaac was finally born to Sarah and Abraham when Abraham was 100 years old and Sarah was 99. That's a long time to wait, believing that God is going to do what he promised! We're told in Romans 4 that Abraham didn't waver in his trust, "fully convinced that God was able to do what he had promised" (Rom. 4:20–21).

6. God tested Abraham. Read James 1:2–3, 13. For what purpose does God allow trials and tests to come our way? What is the difference between a test and a temptation?

7. Read Hebrews 11:12, 17–19. In what ways do you see a direct fulfillment of the promises God made to Abraham in Genesis 15:5 and 22:17?

   a. Based on Hebrews 11:17, fill in the blank: "By _____ Abraham, when he was tested, [obeyed]."

   b. What conclusion about God did Abraham reach that allowed him to trust and obey? `

8. Read Galatians 3:7–9. Who are Abraham's offspring?

   a. Read Revelation 7:9–10. Who will be included in the "great multitude that no one could number"?

   b. How is this the ultimate fulfillment of God's promise to Abraham?

   c. Whom will they be worshiping?

How Does the Text Transform Me?

The account of God telling Abraham to sacrifice Isaac is unique in Scripture. F. B. Meyers said, "There is only one scene in history by which it is surpassed: that where the Great Father gave His Isaac to a death from which there was no deliverance."[1] On the one hand, if the sacrifice of Isaac had been made, it would have been an awful scene full of horror and heartbreak. But the sacrifice of Isaac was dramatically stopped, and the scene was turned into one of the most powerful and beautiful pictures of the cost to the Father in the completed sacrifice of his Son. Jesus did not receive a substitute. He died as *our* substitute.

As you spend time today thinking about how you can apply this text to your own heart, mind, and life, remember—even though we learn a lot from Abraham, we don't identify with him in the story. We're Isaac, the one who should have died and yet was spared because the Lord provided himself a sacrifice in our place.

READ GENESIS 22:1–19

1. As you consider this story, how does it help you better understand your salvation in Christ?

---

[1] F. B. Meyer and Lance Wubbels, *The Life of Abraham: The Obedience of Faith* (Lynnwood: YWAM Pub, 1996), 167.

2. In what ways have you seen God's provision in the midst of trials and testing?

This story is not primarily about Abraham and his obedience—it's about God and his provision. And yet, based on this story, we can see that obedience is crucial in the life of a believer. The question we should all ask is, *What role does obedience have in my life?*

It's easy for us to read a story like this, or the one last week, and think that God saves/loves us if we obey him. But that is not how it works! God saves us because he loves us, because he's merciful, and because Jesus obeyed in our place. And *then*, because God is loving, merciful, and kind, we trust him, and he gives us the desire to obey. Obedience demonstrates our love for God; it's not the reason we receive his love.

Both James and Paul write that Abraham's obedience was a direct result of his faith. The order is really important. God, in his sovereign wisdom and mercy, gave Abraham faith and then counted Abraham as righteous for having that faith. Abraham was not counted as righteous because of his obedience but because of his faith. Then, as a result of his faith, Abraham obeyed God.

3. Is there anything the Lord is currently asking you to obey? How does your love of God compel you?

4. Abraham obeyed even when it seemed to make no sense. He trusted that God was going to work it out somehow. Is there a circumstance in your life where you can trust that God will work it out even if you don't know how or when? What might be standing in the way of your trust?

5. Spend some time thinking about how difficult it must have been for Abraham to walk up that mountain believing he was going to sacrifice his beloved son. This story gives us a window of understanding into the choice God made to sacrifice his only Son on our behalf.

    a. In what ways are you tempted to doubt God's love for you today?

    b. What does this story tell you about God's love for you?

    c. Take the time to write out the ways God's love for you is evident in your life.

6. In Romans 8:31–32 Paul asked, "If God is for us, who can be against us?" and if he willingly gave up his Son, "how will he not also with him graciously give us all things?"

    a. What circumstances in your life today might cause you to doubt that God is for you?

    b. In what ways are you tempted to think that God is withholding something good from you?

c. In what ways does remembering the cross change your view of those circumstances? How can you remind yourself of these two truths (God is for me; God is good to me) throughout the day today?

7. How does this account of Abraham and Isaac encourage you to believe, live, or love differently as a result of your study this week?

When I was 7, my dad decided to learn to fly an airplane. I remember his first solo flight (probably due more to the tradition of cutting off the back of the new pilot's shirt than anything about the actual event). For the next few years, he could only fly if he was able to actually see where he was going. He would fly over major interstates so that he wouldn't get lost. If it was cloudy or overcast, he had to postpone his flight.

When I was 9, he received his instrument rating. This allowed him to fly even when he couldn't physically see where he was going. His instruments would tell him where he was and help him navigate from point A to point B. He said it was hard to learn to trust the instruments and not rely on sight.

Paul tells us in 2 Corinthians that we are to "walk by faith, not by sight" (5:7). In the same way it was hard for my dad to learn to trust the instruments in his plane, it's hard for us to walk in faith when we can't see where our path is headed. One thing we learn from Abraham is that the ability to walk in faith, even when we can't see the outcome, is only possible when we trust in the character of our good God.

Before Abraham and Sarah had any children, God changed Abram's name (meaning "exalted father") to Abraham ("father of a multitude"). He promised Abraham would have offspring as numerous as the stars in the heavens and the sand on the shore. Abraham believed God would do what he said he would do. However, it wasn't until Abraham was 100 years old that Isaac, the promised child, was born. What joy, what delight, and what love they must have felt!

I have no doubt that Isaac brought Sarah and Abraham as much peace as he did joy. As they watched him grow, they were able to rest in the fact that God had done everything he had promised for them. Isaac was tangible evidence that God was going to fulfill all he had said. Isaac would be the firstborn of the multitude spoken of by God.

And, as readers of the story, we should read about the birth of Isaac and realize that it will be through him the offspring promised in Genesis 3:15 will arrive. Such hope rests on Isaac.

And then God asked the unimaginable. He told Abraham to take this child, this child of promise, this only child, this child Abraham loved, and kill him as a sacrifice. As readers, we're kindly given the first verse before we read of this shocking request. We're told that God was testing Abraham. But Abraham didn't know that—yet he obeyed.

In addition to the emotional anguish, Abraham must have also felt the great tension between this clear request and God's earlier promises. If Abraham obeyed and sacrificed the promised offspring, how would God's promises come to pass? The author of Hebrews tells us how Abraham resolved this tension: he believed that God could raise Isaac from the dead! As James Boice points out, "There had never been a resurrection in the history of the world, [but] that doesn't make any difference."[1] Abraham trusted in God's character (that he was good), God's Word (that he was faithful), and God's power (that he was able).

You and I will never face such an unthinkable dilemma. Yet we all face situations when obedience to God's Word seems to make no sense. Or feels too hard. Or costs too much. We just can't see how obeying God could be the best path forward. The author of Proverbs reminds us: "Trust in the LORD with all your heart, and *do not lean on your own understanding*. In all your ways acknowledge him, and he will make straight your paths" (Prov. 3:5–6, emphasis mine). Abraham lived the truth of that proverb long before it was penned.

Abraham knew the character of God, and it compelled him to trust. You and I know so much more about the goodness of God. We know that he loves us so much that he gave his beloved Son for us (John 3:16). We know that nothing can separate us from his steadfast love (Rom. 8:38–39). We know that he is working all things out for the good of those who believe (Rom. 8:28). The question is, will you allow what you know to be true to cultivate deep trust and radical faith in you? As you do, you will be able to walk by faith and not by sight because the Lord himself will provide all you need.

---

[1] James Montgomery Boice, *Genesis: An Expositional Commentary* (Grand Rapids: Zondervan, 1985), 221.

1. What is one thing you learned about God this week?

2. What is one way you hope to change?

3. In what way does this salvation story remind you of the joy of your salvation in Christ?

Icebreaker Question

What is your favorite ingredient substitution when you're cooking (e.g., applesauce for oil)?

Warm-Up Question

Briefly share with your group about a time you had to walk by faith and not by sight.

READ GENESIS 22:1–19

1. What three to five words did you use to describe Abraham and Isaac's obedience? Why?

2. What details of this passage did you notice that linked it so clearly to Jesus's sacrifice on the cross?

3. Did studying Genesis 22 in light of Genesis 3:15 make any difference in your understanding? How so?

4. In what ways has seeing Jesus as the greater Isaac shaped your understanding of your own salvation?

5. How has seeing Abraham's deep trust and radical obedience helped, convicted, or inspired you?

6. On Day 4 (question 6) we asked you to consider Paul's questions in Romans 8:31–32. Share your answers with each other.

7. Share with your group one thing you learned about God this week or one way you hope to change.

8. Share with your group how this salvation story reminds you of the joy of your salvation in Christ.

Water from the Rock

Salvation Is Life

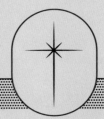

Melissa Kruger

INTRODUCTION

Last week, we studied God's work in the life of Abraham and his son, Isaac. The promised offspring from Genesis would one day come from Abraham's descendants. As the story continued to unfold, Joseph—the son of Jacob (Israel), the son of Isaac—was sold by his brothers into slavery in Egypt. God used their wrong actions (fueled by familial jealousy) to protect Abraham's family from a severe famine in the land (Gen. 50:20). They entered Egypt as a family of 70 people (Ex. 1:5). They left as a nation of more than a million (Num. 2:32).[1]

However, they were not allowed to leave easily. While Joseph had risen to second in command in Pharaoh's house, later generations of Israel were oppressed and enslaved by the Egyptians. As they were subjected to hard labor (Ex. 1:13–14) and the murder of their sons (Ex. 1:16), they cried out to the Lord for relief (Ex. 3:7). God heard their pleas and raised up Moses as a deliverer for his people. God sent plagues to Egypt and worked wonders through Moses and Aaron. Finally, the people of Israel passed through the Red Sea, while Pharaoh and his army were destroyed (Ex. 14:30–31). Miriam (Moses's sister) picked up her tambourine and sang about deliverance (Ex. 15:20–21).

God saved his people (and protected the offspring promised in Genesis), but now they wandered in the wilderness, wondering: *Will God provide?* This week, we'll focus on God's salvation and how he offers us abundant life . . . today.

---

[1] Numbers 2:32 tells us that there were over 600,000 fighting men over the age of 20. However, this did not include the tribe of Levi, nor women and children.

MEMORY VERSE

"'Behold, God is my salvation; I will trust, and will not be afraid; for the LORD GOD is my strength and my song, and he has become my salvation.'
With joy you will draw water from the wells of salvation."

Isaiah 12:2–3

PRAYER FOR THE WEEK

Lord, guide me as I study this passage this week. Open my eyes and let me see wonderous things in your Word. Renew my mind and refresh my heart. Show me where I grumble and complain and do not trust your provision. Give me a soft heart that seeks to do your will.

In Jesus's name I pray. Amen.

What Does the Text Say?

Today we're going to spend our time simply observing the text. Good observation begins by listening to the story and absorbing all the details. Start your time with prayer, and then read the text carefully. If possible, read it out loud. Our study will focus primarily on Exodus 17:1–7, but today we're going to read Exodus 15:22–17:7 to get the full context of the story after the miraculous crossing of the Red Sea.

READ EXODUS 15:22–17:7

1. Go back through the text and observe:

    a. Who are the characters in this story? How are they described?

    b. What happens in the story? Briefly summarize the events in your own words.

    c. Who is saved in this story, and by what means are they saved?

2. Fill in the chart below, listing the need the Israelites faced, their response, and how God provided for their need.

Passage	Need	Israel's Response	God's Provision
Ex. 15:22–27			
Ex. 16			
Ex. 17:1–7			

3. Reread Exodus 15:23, 16:1, and 16:35.

    a. How long had they been in the wilderness at this point?

    b. How much time passed between these two stories?

    c. How long did God provide the manna?

4. Consider Exodus 17:5–7.

    a. Make a list of everything God commands Moses to do.

    b. What does God say he will do in verse 6?

    c. What do the names Massah and Meribah mean (they should be footnoted in your Bible)?

5. Did any details in the story surprise or confuse you? Do you have any questions about the passage?

What Does the Text Mean?

Today we'll spend our time going deeper in our understanding as we seek to interpret the text. Good interpretation flows from thoughtful observation, so take the time to read the passage again. Begin your time with prayer, asking God to give you wisdom as you study.

READ EXODUS 15:22–17:7

1. What do you learn about God in this passage?

2. What do you learn about mankind?

3. In what ways do the Israelites have an overly fond remembrance of their time in Egypt? What do they remember about their time there? What have they forgotten?

4. Why is water so important? Write out four to five uses of water in your daily life.

5. Numbers 2:32 tells us there were more than 600,000 men older than 20 who left Egypt. We can assume there were more than a million Israelites (most likely more than 2 million) who needed water to drink. If God had not provided manna and water for the Israelites, what would have happened to them? How does the number of people needing water affect the image you have of the amount of water than came out of the rock?

6. Read Exodus 7:14–25.

   a. Which plague was this for the Egyptians?

   b. What did God command Moses to do? Why?

   c. What happened when the staff struck the water (v. 20)?

   d. Compare this passage to Exodus 17:1–7. What similarities do you notice? What differences?

7. When Moses struck the Nile and it turned to blood, it was God's judgment on Pharaoh's hard heart and unwillingness to let the people of God go. In the Exodus 17 passage, who deserves God's judgment?

8. Read Psalm 78:17–20, 35–38.

    a. What do you learn about the Israelites from this passage?

    b. What do you learn about God?

    c. Why is it significant that God is called their rock?

What Does the New Testament Say?

Today we'll spend our time going deeper in our understanding as we seek to interpret the text by reading a few New Testament passages that reference this passage. Good interpretation flows from thoughtful observation, so take the time to read these passages and consider them in light of Exodus 15–17. Begin your time with prayer, asking God to give you wisdom as you study.

READ EXODUS 17:1-7

1. Read John 6:47–51. How is Jesus's description of himself similar to God's provision in Exodus 16?

2. Read John 4:7–15. Give three descriptions of the water Jesus offers.

3. Read Jeremiah 2:13.

   a. How does God describe himself?

b. What are the two evils God's people have done?

c. How is this passage similar to what Jesus says in John 4?

4. Read John 7:2, 37–39.

   a. What feast was being celebrated? What did that feast represent (see Lev. 23:42–43)?

   b. What invitation does Jesus offer? To whom? In what ways is this invitation similar to Isaiah 55:1–3?

   c. According to these verses, what does the living water represent?

5. Read 1 Corinthians 10:1–4. What do you learn about the rock in Exodus from this passage?

6. Read Matthew 26:67, Mark 15:19, Luke 22:64, and John 19:3. What common word do you notice in each of these passages that is also in Exodus 17?

7. Consider these three words: rock, struck, and water. How did the rock being struck to produce water save the Israelites? How does this imagery point to our greater salvation in Christ? Who was struck, and what did it provide for our salvation?

How Does the Text Transform Me?

We've observed the text and interpreted its meaning. Now it's time to take what we've studied and apply it to our own lives. Pray for the Spirit to transform you as you study God's Word today.

READ EXODUS 17:1–7

1. As you consider this story, how does it help you better understand your salvation in Christ?

2. The Israelites struggled to trust God in the wilderness, even though he provided for them time and time again. In what ways are you struggling to trust in God today? How can remembering his past faithfulness help you trust him in present circumstances? Take a few minutes to read Psalm 77, and use it to guide you in prayer.

3. Are there any areas of your life where you regularly grumble or complain? Confess any discontentment you are struggling with to the Lord (and maybe a trusted friend). Prayerfully ask him to give you a heart of gratitude and trust.

4. Read 1 Corinthians 10:1–13. How do Old Testament stories serve to instruct us today? What warning should you heed in verse 12, and what encouragement do you find in verse 13?

5. The images of water and bread point to our daily need for Jesus. When we don't eat or drink, we often find ourselves feeling physically unwell or weary. What are spiritual signs in your life that you need time in the presence of Jesus? In what ways have you seen time in Jesus's presence refresh and revive you?

6. Read Isaiah 12:1–3. What do you think it means to say, "with joy you will draw water from the wells of salvation"? What would that look like in your life? How does the good news of your salvation offer you joy today?

7. How does the story of God's faithful provision of water to the Israelites encourage you to believe, live, or love differently as a result of your study this week?

I woke up this morning and did what I always do. I put toothpaste on my toothbrush and turned on the faucet to brush my teeth. Next, I put my contacts in and rinsed out the case. Afterwards, I turned on my shower and watched with little amazement or surprise as clean water flowed out effortlessly.

Most days, I take for granted how easy it is to have clean water. However, in many places in the world, women spend more than four hours a day trying to find water—and usually the water they find isn't clean. Diseases from unhealthy water kill more people each year than wars or any form of violence.[1] Clean water—something that is so easy for those of us with access to it to take for granted—is a basic necessity for life.

When I picture more than a million Israelites wandering in the desert and thirsting for something to drink, I can sympathize with their despair. They rightly understood their physical needs—they knew without water they would die. However, their biggest problem wasn't their lack of water. Their biggest problem was their lack of faith. Even though they'd seen God's miracles in Egypt, they didn't understand the covenant love or the character of the God who had called them out of slavery to life.

Their unbelief overflowed into faithless grumbling and complaining. God welcomes us when we cry out to him in our distress. However, a sinful, discontented complaint reveals our lack of trust. As Puritan preacher Thomas Watson explained, "Here is the difference between a *holy* complaint and a *discontented* complaint; in one we complain *to* God; in the other we complain *of* God."[2] He also wisely warned,

---

[1] "Global Water Crisis," Charity: Water, accessed October 13, 2020, https://www.charitywater.org/global-water-crisis.

[2] Thomas Watson, *The Art of Divine Contentment* (Soli Deo Gloria Ministries, 2001), https://www.monergism.com/thethreshold/sdg/watson/The%20Art%20of%20Divine%20Contentment%20-%20Thomas%20Watson.pdf.

"Discontent is nothing else but the echo of unbelief. Remember *distrust* is worse than *distress*."[3]

While I may not be as familiar with physical thirst, I know what it's like to thirst for more in this life. Sin can seem like the more delightful path—enticing as those pots of meat the Israelites were craving. In remembering the pleasures of Egypt, they forgot the pain of their bondage. They also forgot the goodness of their God. I can too easily do the same.

Even if you're not physically thirsty today, there's most likely something in your life that isn't going the way you hoped or planned. You may scan the horizon and only see a barren desert of unfulfilled longings. In the midst of your deep aches and painful thirst, can I tell you the good news? You are invited:

> Come, all you who are thirsty, come to the waters; and you who have no money, come, buy and eat! Come, buy wine and milk without money and without cost. Why spend money on what is not bread, and your labor on what does not satisfy? Listen, listen to me, and eat what is good, and your soul will delight in the richest of fare. Give ear and come to me; hear me, that your soul may live. (Isa. 55:1–3, NIV-84)

Notice who is invited . . . it's not everyone. It's the thirsty. The weary. The aching. The disappointed. The lonely. You. You're invited to come receive wine and milk (even better than water!) and have your soul delight in the richest of feasts. You're invited to life . . . today.

Yes, there's a future bounty of everlasting goodness for those who love Jesus. One day there will be no more suffering and no more tears. But there's also life for the thirsty today. Here's the beautiful reality of our salvation: we're not just saved for eternal life; we're saved for abundant life in Jesus now (John 10:10).

By reminding ourselves what Christ has done on our behalf, we drink with joy from the well of salvation. Just like the Israelites, we've grumbled and complained. We've walked in sinful unbelief. And yet,

---

[3] Watson, *The Art of Divine Contentment*

rather than strike us with punishment, God has shown us mercy. Christ, the rock of our salvation, was struck on our behalf. His body was broken so that the life-giving Spirit could be poured out on all who believe. Do you see the beauty of this glorious exchange? He was struck so that we might live. And that life begins today as the Spirit dwells in us (Rom. 8:11).

Jesus is the bread of life and the fount of living waters. Don't take for granted our free access to this life-giving nourishment. When we're spiritually dry and aching with longings, we don't have to dig our own cisterns, looking for waters that can never quench our thirst. We go to Jesus with our longings, our hurts, our troubles, and our thirst, knowing that he alone can satisfy. Seek him today, trusting with David: "You make known to me the path of life; in your presence there is fullness of joy; at your right hand are pleasures forevermore" (Ps. 16:11).

1. What is one thing you learned about God this week?

2. What is one way you hope to change?

3. In what way does this salvation story remind you of the joy of your salvation in Christ?

Icebreaker Question

What is your favorite drink?

Warm-Up Question

Can anyone share about a time when you were
extremely hungry or thirsty? What was it like? How did it
make you act differently from normal?

READ EXODUS 17:1–7

1. Take some time to discuss as a group all the ways you've used
   water already today. Why might the Israelites have been so fearful
   of their lack of water?

2. How did the Israelites' grumbling and complaining flow from a lack
   of belief in God? How does our own grumbling and complaining
   result from unbelief? What is the difference between "complaining
   to God" and "complaining about God"?

3. Compare this account to how the staff brought death and destruction on the Egyptians in Exodus 7:14–25. How does this story foreshadow Christ taking the punishment for our sin?

4. On Day 4, question 4, you were asked to read 1 Corinthians 10:1–13. How do Old Testament stories instruct us today? What warning should you heed in verse 12, and what encouragement do you find in verse 13?

5. The images of water and bread point to our daily need for Jesus. When we don't eat or drink, we often feel physically unwell or weary. What are spiritual signs in your life that you need time in the presence of Jesus? How have you seen time in Jesus's presence refresh and revive you? Why is it so easy to take time with Jesus for granted?

6. Read Isaiah 12:1–3. What do you think it means to say, "with joy you will draw water from the wells of salvation"? What would that look like in your life? How does the good news of your salvation offer you joy today?

7. Share with your group one thing you learned about God this week. Also share one thing you learned about your own heart, mind, or life, or one way you hope to change.

8. Share with your group how this salvation story reminds you of the joy of your salvation in Christ.

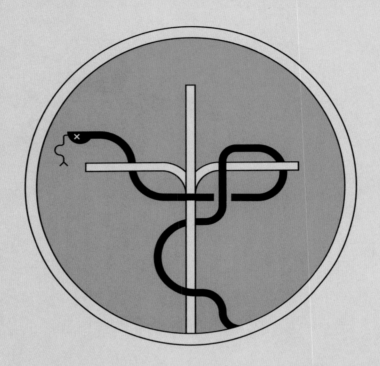

Serpent on the Pole

Salvation Is Gracious

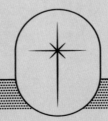

Courtney Doctor

INTRODUCTION

In last week's study, the hungry and thirsty Israelites grumbled, complained, and questioned the goodness of God—and the Lord graciously and miraculously provided food and water for them in the desert. This week, we're going to jump ahead in the story, but you'll notice many unfortunate similarities.

Numbers, the fourth book of the Bible, chronicles the Israelites from the time they left Egypt through their 40 years of desert wandering. After God miraculously delivered them *from* Egypt, they didn't believe he would deliver them *into* the promised land (Num. 13–14). As a consequence of their disbelief and disobedience, God required them to wander around the desert for 40 years, until the generation of those who hadn't believed were dead. The passage we're studying this week is the first story told about that second generation—and we'll see that they were not much different from their parents. They were grumblers, complainers, and doubters, too.

It's a strange story—the serpent on the pole—and it's probably less familiar than the other ones we've studied so far. It might strike us (no pun intended) as odd on several levels. You may wonder why God sent serpents to bite the people. Or, in light of Genesis 3:15, why he chose a serpent as the image they looked at to be saved. Hopefully, by the end of the week, we'll have answers to some of those questions.

As you study this week, I hope you will see the mercy and grace of God in new ways. He is the One who graciously provides life for all who will look to him in faith.

MEMORY VERSE

"And the LORD said to Moses, 'Make a fiery serpent and set it on a pole, and everyone who is bitten, when he sees it, shall live.'"

Numbers 21:8

PRAYER FOR THE WEEK

Lord, I bow before you and acknowledge that my ways are not your ways. Your ways are higher, better, and infinitely wiser than mine. Teach me to trust you, look to you, and delight in the mercy and grace you have shown me in your Son.

In Jesus's name I pray. Amen.

What Does the Text Say?

We'll begin this week the same way we've begun the others—by observing the text. Remember to read slowly, paying attention and absorbing all the details you find. Begin your time with prayer, and then read the text carefully. If possible, read it out loud.

READ NUMBERS 21:4-9

1. Go back through the text and observe:

    a. Who are the characters in this story? How are they described?

    b. What happens in the story? Briefly summarize the story in your own words.

    c. Who is saved in this story, and by what means are they saved?

2. What does verse 4 say about the people?

3. What is ironic about verse 5?

4. What was good about how the people responded in verse 7?

5. What did the people tell Moses to ask for in prayer? Is that what God did?

6. Who was to look at the pole?

7. Did any details in the story surprise or confuse you? Do you have any questions about the passage?

What Does the Text Mean?

Remembering that we're tracing the seed of the woman and the seed of the serpent makes this week's passage even more interesting! Today, we'll spend our time going deeper in our understanding as we seek to interpret the text. Good interpretation flows from thoughtful observation, so take the time to read the passage again today. Begin your time with prayer, asking God to give you wisdom as you study.

READ NUMBERS 21:4–9

1.   What do you think was so offensive to God about the Israelites' behavior and attitudes?

As you saw last week, complaining about manna was a common occurrence in the 40 years of desert wanderings. Let's review what manna was and when it was provided.

2. Briefly read Exodus 16 and fill in the chart below.

v. 1	How long had the people been out of Egypt when God provided the manna?	
vv. 2–3	What did the people accuse Moses and Aaron of doing?	
v. 7	What were the people supposed to see when they saw the manna?	
v. 12	What were the people to know when they saw the manna?	
vv. 16-18	What do we learn about the sufficiency of the manna?	
v. 31	What did it taste like?	

3. In what ways does Exodus 16 compare to verses 4–5 of this week's passage?

   a. "And the people became impatient on the way."

   b. "And the people spoke against God and against Moses, 'Why have you brought us up out of Egypt to die in the wilderness?'"

   c. "there is no food and no water"

   d. "we loathe this worthless food"

4. How do you think God wanted Israel to respond to and receive his provision?

5. Why do you think it might be significant that God sent fiery serpents?

I wish I could read what you just wrote! Why *did* God send serpents, of all things, and why did God have Moses put a serpent on a pole as the means of salvation from sure death? We've most likely all been asking these questions as we study this week. We'll begin to answer the first of those questions today, and we'll tackle the second one tomorrow.

As we said in the introduction, in the story of redemption the serpent (Satan) continually wages war against the promised seed of the woman. There have been times in history when the battle became a visible, raging war. For instance, when Herod killed all the baby boys in Bethlehem (Matt. 2:16), Revelation 12 tells us that this horror was a part of this epic battle. The Devil himself attempted to kill the seed of the woman through the evil intentions of those whose hearts were hardened.

More than 1,000 years before Herod tried to kill all the baby boys in Bethlehem, Pharaoh tried to kill all the Israelite baby boys. Interestingly, the pharaohs of Egypt often had a serpent, or the head of a serpent, on their crown to represent their power. In light of the great story of redemption, the serpent was an appropriate choice for the person who represented the power that oppressed and killed God's people. The ancient serpent is always set against God's people.

One reason God might have sent snakes as a punishment to the grumbling Israelites was to remind them of the oppression they had endured at the hand of the one who wore the serpent. When the Israelites acted as if they had it so much better in Egypt, God sent serpents to remind them of the far greater suffering he had delivered them from. And, just like God had done in Egypt, he again showed them he was the One who could save them from the sure death the serpents brought.

6. God could have had anyone who wanted to *avoid* a snake bite look at the serpent on the pole. Why do you think he wanted those who had *already been bitten* to look?

7. We'll go further into this question tomorrow, but why do you think God might have had the people look at a representation of the very thing that was killing them?

8. What do you learn about God in this passage, and what do you learn about mankind?

What Does the New Testament Say?

Yesterday, we briefly began to answer the first part of our question: why did God send serpents? Today, I want us to consider why God might have told Moses to put a serpent on a pole as the means of salvation from sure death.

   Open your time in prayer, asking for wisdom to read and understand this story in light of the bigger story of Scripture.

1. Read Matthew 4:1–4.

    a. Where is Jesus?

    b. What condition is he in and why (v. 2)? How is this different from what the Israelites faced in the desert?

    c. Who comes to him, and what does he say?

    d. How does Jesus do what the Israelites failed to do?

2. In John 3:14–15, Jesus tells Nicodemus, "And as Moses lifted up the serpent in the wilderness, so must the Son of Man be lifted up, that whoever believes in him may have eternal life."

   a. Who is to be lifted up? When do you think this happened?

   b. What would happen as a result of him being lifted up?

   c. List any similarities and differences you see between the passage in Numbers 21 and what Jesus told Nicodemus in this passage.

3. Read the following verses and answer the questions below:

Romans 6:23: "For the wages of sin is death, but the free gift of God is eternal life in Christ Jesus our Lord."

2 Corinthians 5:21: "For our sake he made him to be sin who knew no sin, so that in him we might become the righteousness of God."

   a. What does sin justly earn a person (what are the wages of sin)?

   b. Even though Jesus never sinned, what did God allow Jesus to represent?

c. What is the free gift God gives in his Son?

In the same way the Israelites had to look at the thing that was killing them hanging on a pole, so we too have to look upon what kills us.

4. Read John 6:35–41.

   a. What does Jesus call himself in verse 35?

   b. Who receives eternal life?

   c. Who is raised up?

   d. How do the Jews respond to Jesus? How is their response similar to their ancestors?

5. Read 1 Corinthians 10:9–11 and Hebrews 3:7–9.

    a. Whom did the Israelites put to the test?

    b. What three things are we told not to do?

6. What does it mean to put Christ to the test? Why is it a sign of a heart that has gone astray?

7. Read Hebrews 7:25. How did Moses show us an aspect of Jesus's ministry in Numbers 21? What comfort does this offer you?

The Israelites had continually rebelled and grumbled against the God who had saved them. They didn't deserve his provision; they deserved his wrath. They didn't deserve his favor; they deserved his judgment. But that's the point. Grace is the love and favor of God given freely to those who don't deserve it. We don't earn God's grace. We receive it—gratefully.

Just as the salvation from sure death offered to the Israelites in the desert was based solely on God's unmerited favor and love, so our salvation is too.

8. In light of Jesus, how do you see God's provision of the serpent on the pole as gracious?

Jesus was lifted up on the cross, bearing the entire weight of the sin that causes our eternal death. It was on the cross that he, the One promised in Genesis 3:15, fulfilled what God spoke so long ago—he crushed the head of the enemy. So, look to Jesus! You will find healing from the deadly venom of the ancient serpent. You will not die in the wilderness. You will live.

How Does the Text Transform Me?

READ NUMBERS 21:4-9

Today, we'll begin to ask how this story is meant to transform us. When we study Scripture, we always want to be asking what we are to know, believe, love, or do differently as a result of what we see and learn. Ask the Lord to help you not just be a hearer of the Word, but to apply the truths to your own life.

1. As you consider this story, how does it help you better understand your salvation in Christ?

The Israelites had been slaves under cruel taskmasters in Egypt. They were beaten, oppressed, and made to do heavy labor (Ex. 1:11–14). For a time, their sons were systematically killed as soon as they were born (Ex. 1:16). Egypt was a horrible place for the Israelites.

We're told that "the people of Israel groaned because of their slavery and cried out for help" (Ex. 2:23). God heard and came down with miracles and displays of his mighty power to rescue and deliver his people (Ex. 4–14). They were free, rescued, and delivered!

But, as you saw last week, those same people—the ones who had just been delivered from slavery—grumbled and complained that God had rescued them just to (supposedly) kill them in the desert. God, so patient and gracious, again provided for them. This time it was bread and water. Years later, in spite of the fact that God had continued to provide for them, we see they were still grumbling and complaining and asking, "Why have you brought us up out of Egypt to die in the wilderness?" (Num. 21:5).

2. In what ways can we do the same thing? Are you ever tempted to return to your former way of life, thinking it was better and forgetting that you were a slave to sin?

One commentator says, "They forget, on the one hand, the terrible conditions under which they had labored as slaves in Egypt, and, on the other hand, the fact that they are journeying towards a land 'flowing with milk and honey'. The former reflects their lack of gratitude for all that God has done for them in the past, and the latter displays their lack of faith regarding all God will do for them in the future."[1] Oh, we can be like those Israelites!

3. In verse 5, the phrase "spoke against" can also be translated "grumbled." As you consider your life, in what areas are you most likely to grumble and complain? In what ways does our grumbling "speak against" God?

4. In what ways have you seen grumbling spread, from person to person and from generation to generation? Why is it so important that we guard what we say (and even think) in our workplaces and homes?

---

[1] T. D. Alexander, *From Paradise to the Promised Land: An Introduction to the Pentateuch* (Grand Rapids: Baker Academic, 2002), 244.

5. Using the chart below, make a list of three to four things God has delivered you from and three to four things God is currently providing for you. Spend some time journaling a prayer of thanksgiving below.

God has delivered me from . . .	God is currently providing me with . . .

6. In what ways might you be testing God's patience (1) by complaining about what he has given or (2) by coveting something he has chosen not to give (e.g., certain spiritual gifts, a spouse, a career, children, ministry opportunities, financial freedom, a bigger home, physical beauty, a different life)?

7. If you had been an Israelite bitten by a snake in this story, do you think it would have been hard to believe and look at the serpent on the pole? Why or why not? Is it ever hard to look to Christ in faith when you sin? Why or why not?

8. When we look at our lives, it's easy to fall into grumbling and complaining. How would daily "looking to Jesus" (Heb. 12:2) and considering his benefits help foster contentment? Spend some time writing out the ways God has blessed you spiritually in Jesus. (See Ephesians 1 and Colossians 1 for help.)

Approximately 600 years after the events of this passage, we read that Hezekiah "broke in pieces the bronze serpent that Moses had made, for until those days the people of Israel had made offerings to it (it was called Nehushtan)" (2 Kings 18:4). The people had not only named the serpent on the pole, they were actively worshiping it.

9. In what ways are you tempted to cling to and love the gifts of God rather than God himself? Why?

10. How are you encouraged to believe, live, or love differently as a result of your study this week?

May our lives be characterized by gratitude for all the Lord has done, is doing, and will do. And when we stumble and grumble, may we look to Jesus, the One lifted up for our sake.

Years ago, on a vacation to Quebec, our family stayed in a charming bed and breakfast in the old part of the city. The door to each room had a hook on the outside of it, and we were thrilled to find out why. Every morning, a basket filled with butter, jelly, cheese, and fresh croissants from the bakery down the street was hanging on the hook. We quickly learned to wake up, bring the basket in, and enjoy the warm, fresh, and delicious bread inside.

On our way home to Kansas, my daughters asked their father if he would put a hook on the outside of their bedroom door at home. I had to quickly burst their bubble and tell them that even if there were a hook, there would be no basket of goodies hanging on it each morning. But I loved their ingenuity. The idea of walking out my front door every morning and having fresh, warm bread sounded delightful.

As I read the story this week, however, I have to question if I would remain delighted and grateful for long. I hate to admit how much like the Israelites I actually am. When I read that God had provided them with fresh, delicious, and *miraculous* bread every day for approximately 14,600 days—bread that kept them from starving—AND THEY STILL COMPLAINED ABOUT IT, I have to be self-aware enough to recognize the same tendency in myself.

Have you, like me, ever said, "I don't have anything to wear," when, in reality you have an entire closet full of clothes? Or have you opened a full pantry and said, "There's nothing in this house to eat."? When I was beginning my adult life, I used to think, *All I want in life is to have a garage and a laundry room.* I can't remember why those were so high on the list, but when both of those things became mine, the list of "all I want" simply changed and grew to include other things.

This tendency toward discontentment, complaining, and grumbling is like a cancer to our bones. Desire for what we don't have and lack of gratitude for what we do have will eat away at our relationships and, most importantly, our intimacy with God. As James tells us, "desire when it has conceived gives birth to sin, and sin when it is fully grown brings forth death" (James 1:15).

When I was in my 20s, a wise older woman counseled me to develop the discipline of gratitude. She told me to make lists—not just mentally, but in writing—of the things I was grateful for. She encouraged me to remember what the Lord had done as well as recognize what he was currently doing. As I incorporated this wisdom into my life, I was better able to spot when discontentment reared its ugly head and combat it with the truth.

The truth for all of us who are in Christ is that we, like the Israelites, have been delivered from oppression and slavery (Rom. 6:18), and God has provided everything we need for life and godliness (2 Pet. 1:3). He is using all things (Rom. 8:28) to do a good work in us (Phil. 1:6). Our role is to believe him, trust him, and thank him.

Sadly, we fail to do this. But here's the unbelievably good news: Jesus took our discontentment, our grumbling, and our lack of gratitude on himself. He went to the cross knowing that we would forget, we would complain, and we would grow apathetic and bored—even with the salvation he provides. Our hope is not in looking to ourselves. Our only hope is to look on him, the One bearing all our sin and shame, and live.

Ephesians 2:8 says that "by grace you have been *saved* through *faith*. And this is not your own doing; it is the gift of God" (emphasis mine). It was true for the Israelites, and it is true for us. Acts 4:12 tells us "there is salvation in no one else, for there is no other name under heaven given among men by which we must be saved." Look at Jesus. He is our God's gracious salvation for everyone who looks to him.

1. What is one thing you learned about God this week?

2. What is one way you hope to change?

3. In what way does this salvation story remind you of the joy of your salvation in Christ?

Icebreaker Question

What's your least favorite thing to eat?

Warm-Up Question

What was the last thing you complained about?

READ NUMBERS 21:4–9

1. After reading this story, why do you think the Israelites' behavior and attitude was so offensive to God?

2. Read 1 Corinthians 10:9–11 and Hebrews 3:7–9. What three things are we told not to do? What does it mean to put Christ to the test?

3. In what ways might you be testing God's patience by complaining about what he has given or by coveting something he has chosen not to give you? In what ways do complaining and grumbling increase your unhappiness?

4. In what ways have you seen grumbling spread, from person to person and from generation to generation? Why is it so important that we guard what we say (and even think) in our workplaces and homes?

5. Read Matthew 4:1–4. Compare and contrast this story with the Numbers passage. How did Jesus do what the Israelites failed to do?

6. Read John 3:14–15. How does this passage help us to understand Numbers 21:4–9 in light of the larger story of redemption? How does the serpent on the pole foreshadow Christ?

7. Share with your group one thing you learned about God this week.

8. Share with your group one thing you learned about your own heart, mind, life, or one way you hope to change.

Scarlet Cord

Salvation Is for All People

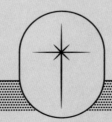

Melissa Kruger

INTRODUCTION

While the Israelites were wandering in the desert—in between the two accounts we studied in chapters 3 and 4—God instructed Moses to send spies to the land of Canaan (Num. 13–14). Moses sent twelve spies, one for each tribe of Israel, and they returned with a glowing but fear-filled report. The spies spoke with wonder about the land of Canaan—it was flowing with milk and honey! However, the bulk of their report was full of fear—the people of Canaan were strong, and their cities were fortified. From what they could see, victory against such a strong foe seemed impossible. Once again, the people responded to this report with faithless cries to return to Egypt.

Yet, two of the spies—Caleb and Joshua—pleaded with the people with eyes of faith:

> The land, which we passed through to spy it out, is an exceedingly good land. If the LORD delights in us, he will bring us into this land and give it to us, a land that flows with milk and honey. Only do not rebel against the LORD. And do not fear the people of the land, for they are bread for us. Their protection is removed from them, and the LORD is with us; do not fear them. (Num. 14:8–9)

Instead of listening, the people responded by picking up rocks to stone them. For their lack of faith, God declared that none of the men who had seen his signs and wonders in Egypt would enter the promised land. After 40 years of wandering, only Joshua and Caleb would be allowed to cross the Jordan and take possession of the land.

In this week's study, we're at the end of those 40 years and the Israelites are on the banks of the Jordan, preparing to enter the promised land. Like Moses, Joshua sends spies into Canaan, and in this story, we learn another beautiful reality about salvation: it's not just for the physical descendants of Abraham. Salvation is for all people who believe by faith.

MEMORY VERSE

"But Rahab the prostitute and her father's household and all who belonged to her, Joshua saved alive. And she has lived in Israel to this day, because she hid the messengers whom Joshua sent to spy out Jericho."

Joshua 6:25

PRAYER FOR THE WEEK

Father, guide me as I study your Word this week. Give me understanding, wisdom, and insight. May the Holy Spirit convict my heart and show me how to apply these truths. Let me behold the good news of salvation in deeper ways as I study the story of Rahab.

In Jesus's name I pray. Amen.

What Does the Text Say?

Today we're going to spend our time simply observing the text. Good observation begins with listening to the story and absorbing all the details. Begin your time with prayer, and then read the text carefully. If possible, read it out loud.

READ JOSHUA 2:1–24; 6:20–25

1. Go back through the text and observe:

   a. Consider the characters in this story. How are they described?

   - Joshua

   - Spies

   - Rahab

   - King of Jericho

   b. What happens in the story? Briefly summarize the story in your own words.

c. Who is saved in this story, and by what means are they saved?

2. How did Rahab respond to the king of Jericho's request (2:3–5)?

3. What did Rahab tell the spies she knew about their God? What did she tell them about her own people (2:9–11)?

4. Who did Rahab ask the spies to save (2:12–13)?

5. How did the spies respond to her request? What specific instructions did they give Rahab (2:14, 17–20)?

6. What did the spies report back to Joshua (2:23–24)?

7. In Joshua 6, what happened to all the inhabitants of Jericho? What happened to Rahab?

8. Think back over this text. What two specific things were accomplished by this mission?

9. Did any details in the story surprise or confuse you? Do you have any questions about the passage?

What Does the Text Mean?

Today we'll spend our time going deeper in our understanding as we seek to interpret the text. Good interpretation flows from thoughtful observation, so take the time to read the passage again. Begin your time with prayer, asking God to give you wisdom as you study.

READ NUMBERS 21:4–9

1. What do you learn about God in this passage?

2. Moses spoke some of his last words to the Israelites just before they crossed the Jordan River. Read Deuteronomy 9:1–6. Consider what you learn about mankind from this passage, as well as Joshua 2.

    a. What do you learn about the inhabitants of Jericho?

    b. Why did God destroy them?

c. What do you learn about the Israelites?

d. Why did God give the Israelites victory?

3. How is this story similar to Noah's ark? In what ways do we see both God's judgment and also his salvation?

4. What do you think Joshua was hoping to accomplish by sending the spies to Jericho? How was God at work in ways that Joshua didn't know about?

5. Was Rahab wrong to lie to her leaders about the location of the spies?

6. In what ways do you see Rahab's kindness and consideration in this story, both to the spies and also to her family?

7. Consider Exodus 12:13, 22–23. What similarities do you see between these two stories?

8. The spies return home and report Rahab's information to Joshua. In what ways would their report have encouraged Joshua to "be strong and courageous" (Josh. 1:9)?

9. What would have happened to Rahab if Joshua hadn't sent the spies to Jericho?

What Does the New Testament Say?

Today we'll spend our time going deeper in our understanding as we seek to interpret the text by reading a few New Testament passages that tell us more about the life of Rahab. Good interpretation flows from thoughtful observation, so take the time to read these passages and consider them in light of Joshua 2. Begin your time with prayer, asking God to give you wisdom as you study.

1. Read Matthew 1:1–16, noting verses 5 and 6.

    a. Who was Rahab's husband?

    b. Who was her son?

    c. Who was her daughter-in-law? Was she an Israelite (see Ruth 1:4)?

    d. Who was Rahab's grandson?

e. Who was Rahab's great-great-grandson (v. 6)?

f. Eventually, who is the greatest descendant of Rahab (v. 16)?

2. Consider what you know about the story of Ruth. How do you think having Rahab as his mother affected Boaz? How did Boaz display kindness and welcome Ruth, even though she was an outsider (see Ruth 2:8–16; 4:9–17)?

3. As you consider the theme of this week (salvation is for all people), why do you think it's significant that Rahab becomes great-great-grandmother to David and is part of Christ's genealogy?

4. Hebrews 11 is sometimes referred to as the "Hall of Faith" because it recounts the faithful deeds of many Old Testament saints. Skim over this chapter and read Hebrews 11:31.

a. Why did Rahab welcome the spies?

b. List out a few reasons it might be surprising for Rahab to be included in this chapter.

5. Read James 2:20–26.

   a. Which two individuals are commended for their good works in this passage?

   b. Why do you think James chose Abraham as an example of the importance of works in displaying the faith of the individual?

   c. Why is it surprising that James uses Rahab as an example? Why is it important that he chose to do so?

I know the passage in James can seem confusing. It might sound like he is saying that our works are the reason for our salvation, rather than the product of our salvation. However, words can mean different things in different contexts. In the apostle Paul's writings, justification usually means "to declare a person righteous." In this sense, we are justified by grace alone, through faith alone. We are declared righteous solely on the merits of Christ's work for our salvation. However, James seems to be using the word differently. In the context of his overall argument, he uses the term justification to mean "to be shown or proven righteous" by our actions. In this sense, our actions demonstrate our faith. Good works are not the basis of salvation, but they display a living and active faith.

I can tell you my name is Melissa Kruger, but if you asked me to prove it, I would have to pull out a passport or marriage certificate to justify to you that it is my actual name. Does my passport make me Melissa Kruger? Not in the least! However, it does prove to others that is my name. My passport justifies that I am Melissa Kruger, but I was declared to be Melissa Kruger when I married my husband 23 years ago.

Just as there was a moment in my wedding that I was declared to be Melissa Kruger, the moment we believe by faith, we are united with Christ and declared righteous. Our works prove that faith is alive in our hearts. Both Abraham (the father of Israel) and Rahab (a foreigner and prostitute) were saved by faith alone, and then their faith was demonstrated in their actions. As John Calvin said, "It is therefore faith alone which justifies, and yet the faith which justifies is not alone."[1]

So, Paul and James do not disagree with each other. Rather, they protect the gospel from two different dangers. Paul is protecting it from legalism (my works save me), and James is protecting it from antinomianism (my works don't matter).

6. In what ways does Rahab's story demonstrate God's graciousness to all people—regardless of their nationality, ethnicity, or even previous lifestyle choices?

7. As you consider this story, how does it help you better understand your salvation in Christ?

---

[1] John Calvin, *Acts of the Council of Trent with the Antidote, Canon 11* (1547), https://www.monergism.com/thethreshold/sdg/calvin_tren-tantidote.html.

How Does the Text Transform Me?

We've observed the text and interpreted its meaning. Now it's time to take what we've studied and apply it to our own lives. Pray for the Spirit to transform you as you study God's Word today.

READ JOSHUA 2:1–24; 6:20–25

1. As a commander, Joshua did his duty when he sent the spies to scout out the land. Even though God had promised him victory, he worked with wisdom at his given task. God used Joshua's ordinary faithfulness to accomplish a bigger mission. Joshua didn't know about Rahab, but God did. Have you had times in your life when you were going about your ordinary tasks and God was working in surprising ways? How have you seen God use faithful acts of service or mundane tasks to accomplish his bigger purposes?

2. When she hid the spies, Rahab lied to her leaders in order to protect them. While Rahab is praised for her faith in Hebrews, her falsehood is never praised (nor condemned) in Scripture. Consider Calvin's thoughts on this passage:

   > As to the falsehood, we must admit that though it was done for a good purpose, it was not free from fault. For those who hold what is called a dutiful lie to be altogether excusable, do not sufficiently consider how precious truth is in the sight of God. Therefore, although our purpose be to assist our brethren, to consult for their safety and relieve them, it never can be lawful to lie, because that cannot be right which is contrary to the nature of God. And God is truth. And still the act of Rahab is not devoid of the praise of virtue, although it was not spotlessly pure. For it often happens that while the saints study to hold the right path, they deviate into circuitous courses. [1]

---

[1] John Calvin, *Calvin's Commentaries*, https://ccel.org/ccel/calvin/calcom07/calcom07.v.i.html

a. Do you agree with Calvin's thoughts above? (And, just so you know, other commentators have different opinions about Rahab's actions.) Was her method of protecting the spies wrong? Are there situations where lying or hiding the truth are acceptable (see also Ex. 1:15–21; Judg. 4:17–24; 5:24–27)?

b. In a general sense, we know that lying is wrong (Ex. 20:16). Do you have areas of life where you are hiding the truth from someone, telling partial truths, or perhaps lying outright? If so, confess to the Lord, and if needed, confess to anyone you have wronged.

3. Consider all the Lord did to save Rahab and her family. Somehow, Rahab heard about the miracles God worked among the Israelites. Then, Israelite spies showed up at her door. By faith, she put her trust in God and hid the spies when the king of Jericho was searching for them. The spies promised to protect Rahab and her family. Rahab—a prostitute and foreigner—was plucked out and saved from the coming disaster. Think about your own story. How did God work in your life to save you? List out the various people God used and the ways the Lord rescued you. Then, spend some time praising him for his great kindness to you!

Sometimes, people with certain types of past sins (especially sexual sins) feel like God could never use them—that somehow, the Holy Spirit only really works in people who have a spotless past. Well, Rahab's story is a good reminder of two things. First, no one has a sinless story. Romans 3:10 (NIV-84) says, "There is no one righteous, not even one." Second, when we come to Christ, we are a new creation. In 2 Corinthians 5:17 (NIV-84), Paul assures us, "Therefore, if anyone is in Christ, he is a new creation; the old has gone, the new has come!"

Satan would love to keep you bound in his lies and have you mistakenly believe that Christ's blood is powerful enough to save you, but it is not powerful enough to make you clean or to use you for God's glory. Please stop listening to the lies and remember Rahab. She was a foreigner and a prostitute, and yet she believed in the God of Israel. Her faith is listed in Hebrews 11 alongside Abraham and Moses! She became a part of the Israelite community and bore the seed that would one day be Christ.

4. Take some time to consider your past. Do you have sins in your past that you would be fearful for others to know? Do they make you think you are somehow not able to be used by God? In what ways does Rahab's story encourage you today?

5. Is there anyone in your life that you think is beyond the hope of the gospel? How does the story of Rahab help you consider that person in a new light? Spend some time praying for the people in your life who need the Lord, asking him to have mercy, seek them out, and rescue them from the darkest of circumstances and situations.

6. As you consider this story, how does it help you better understand your salvation in Christ? In what ways does it help you understand that salvation is for all people who believe in God by faith?

7. How does Rahab's life encourage you to believe, live, or love differently as a result of your study this week?

Have you ever had the experience of knowing you'd been rescued? A few years ago, I was on my way to a conference, driving along the interstate. About 30 minutes into my journey, I suddenly lost control of the car. Most likely, something came apart in my front wheel, detaching it from the axle. On my right, an 18-wheeler loomed; to my left, the guardrail. Thankfully, the car veered left, careening into the guardrail at somewhere around 70 miles per hour. My car proceeded to spin a 360 with such force that the water bottle in my console spun through the air, completely stripped of its plastic casing. I came to a stop in the middle of the fast lane, bracing for the impact of another car.

It never came.

As I sat stunned in the front seat, I tried to move my car forward. I had no idea that both my front wheels were detached and going in opposite directions. Slowly, I opened the crushed left door and squeezed out of the car. Two men rushed towards me asking, "Are you OK?"

Taking stock of myself, I only felt a bit of pain in my left knee (something must have hit it during the crash), and I was left in complete amazement that I was alive. A lady who stopped to help, looked at me and said, "I saw the whole thing happen, and I didn't think anyone was getting out of that car." Tears of gratitude welled, and I replied, "I thought the exact same thing." In the midst of an accident that took only seconds, it's amazing how many thoughts you can think. The main one I thought was, "This is it. I am going to die."

I wonder if Rahab felt a similar fear as she heard the various reports about the Israelites. She told the spies that everyone in their community was so afraid that their "hearts melted, and there was no spirit left in any man" (Josh. 2:11). The citizens of Jericho knew destruction was coming. In Deuteronomy 9, the Lord made it clear that it was not because of Israel's righteousness that the Lord gave them victory in

Canaan, but because of the wickedness of the nations that lived there. The destruction that befell the inhabitants of Canaan was a similar judgment to what happened in Noah's generation.

However, before we get to the first battle, we're offered a glimpse into the mercy of God and the great lengths he will go to in order to save his people. Rahab lived in the city of Jericho as a prostitute. The king of Jericho evidently knew her, for he sent her a message personally asking her to bring out the Israelites who had come to spy on his city. Instead of obeying his wishes and aligning herself with the people of Jericho, she chose to put her lot in with the people of Israel.

Rahab's actions demonstrated her faith—she hid the spies and protected them. In turn, she was promised protection by the scarlet cord tied on her window. Only her family escaped destruction. The Gibeonites later avoided death because of a deceptive treaty they made with Joshua, but they were not welcomed into the Israelite community (Josh. 9). They escaped with their lives, but they lived in forced labor and service to the Israelites. Rahab, on the other hand, became a member of the community of faith.

How do we know that Rahab entered into the Israelite community? It's evident from Matthew's genealogy. She married a man named Salmon and gave birth to a son named Boaz. From the story of Ruth, we know that Boaz was a man of good standing in the community. We also know that he married a woman who was not an Israelite. Ruth was a Moabitess who, like Rahab, gave up her people and clung to the God of Israel. Ruth gave birth to Obed, who was the father of Jesse, who was the father of King David. Rahab became the great-grandmother to the king of Israel! An even greater testimony of her life within the covenant community is the fact that she is one of only four women mentioned in the genealogy of Jesus. This story highlights that even in the Old Testament the true children of Abraham were those who had faith in the God of Israel.

Just as God went to great lengths to save Rahab, he went to even greater lengths to save you and me. As Acts 4:12 (NIV-84) tells us, "Salvation is found in no one else, for there is no other name under heaven given to men by which we must be saved." I'm sure that Rahab told all of those she loved to come to her home and find protection under the scarlet cord tied on her window. Christ bids each of us to come and find protection by his blood, mercifully given to all who will call upon his name. While your story may seem unremarkable or mundane, every salvation story is a story of being saved from disaster.

When my husband came to pick me up from the side of the interstate that morning and saw the broken axle, the guardrail, and where the car had landed, he hugged me tight. We both knew I'd been saved from a much more terrible accident. We went to dinner that night, and all we could talk about was how thankful we were. Take some time today to rejoice that God has rescued you from darkness and death and brought you into his kingdom of light and life. Savor your salvation. Don't stop talking about it. Invite others to come and find life in Jesus. He's the best good news the world has ever received—share him with others.

1. What is one thing you learned about God this week?

2. What is one way you hope to change?

3. In what way does this salvation story remind you of the joy of your salvation in Christ?

Icebreaker Question

What's your favorite type of international food?

Warm-Up Question

Have you ever been rescued? Briefly share what happened and how you were helped.

READ JOSHUA 2:1–24; 6:20–25

1. As you read this story, what are some positive and negative details we learn about Rahab?

2. Read Hebrews 11:31 and James 2:20–26. Why is it surprising that she is an example in both of these accounts?

3. How do you think having Rahab as his mother affected Boaz? Consider what you know about the story of Ruth. How did he display kindness and welcome her, even though she was an outsider (see Ruth 2:8–16; 4:9–17)? What do both of these stories tell us about God's plan for salvation?

4. In what ways did Jesus's genealogy affect your understanding of this story? Why is Rahab significant for us all?

5. As a commander, Joshua did his duty when he sent the spies to scout out the land. Even though God had promised him victory, he worked with wisdom at his given task. God used Joshua's ordinary faithfulness to accomplish a bigger mission. Joshua didn't know about Rahab, but God did. Have you ever gone about your ordinary tasks and observed God working in surprising ways? How have you seen God use faithful acts of service or mundane tasks to accomplish his bigger purposes?

6. Review the five symbols of salvation that we've discussed so far in our study. How do these stories point to a rescue from destruction or death? How do these stories tell a bigger story of God keeping his promise in Genesis 3:15? In what ways can we respond to the message of these stories in our lives today?

7. Share one question and answer from this week that was helpful, convicting, or encouraging.

8. Share one thing you learned about God this week.

Sling and Stones

Salvation Is Won by Another

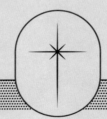

Courtney Doctor

INTRODUCTION

Last week we read that after 400 years in Egypt and 40 years of wandering in the desert, the Israelites were finally about to enter the promised land. With Rahab's help and Joshua's leadership, they crossed the Jordan and began the long process of dividing the land and settling in. Unfortunately, they "settled" a bit too much and ended up following the religious practices of the pagan nations all around them. The book of Judges comes after Joshua, and it's the long, sad account of Israel's downward spiral into idolatry and unbelief. Judges ends with the words, "In those days there was no king in Israel. Everyone did what was right in his own eyes" (Judg. 21:25). *If only we had a king,* they thought, *things might not be so bad.*

The last judge in Israel was Samuel. He anointed and installed Israel's first king, Saul. The people, not God, chose Saul, and God regretted making Saul king (1 Sam. 15:35). Halfway through the book of 1 Samuel we're introduced to a young boy—the youngest of eight sons, a boy from Bethlehem, and the shepherd of his father's sheep—David. Samuel was sent to this boy to anoint him as the future king of Israel.

Eventually, David became the king that all the other kings were compared to. He is called a "man after [God's] own heart" (1 Sam. 13:14; cf. Acts 13:22). David is one of the great heroes of the Old Testament, but he's a mere shadow of our ultimate hero. As we study one of the most epic stories in all of Scripture, I hope you will rejoice anew for all the ways the greater David, Jesus, won the greater battle of our salvation.

MEMORY VERSE

"This day the LORD will deliver you into my hand, and I will strike you down and cut off your head. . . . that all the earth may know that there is a God in Israel"

1 Samuel 17:46

PRAYER FOR THE WEEK

Father, I bow before you and your living Word. Would you give me eyes to see, a mind to understand, and a heart willing to obey? Thank you for sending your Son to do for us what we could never do for ourselves. Help me to rest and rejoice in the salvation he has won for us.

In Jesus's name I pray. Amen.

What Does the Text Say?

By now you know that today we're going to spend our time simply observing the text. This story is a bit longer, so take your time, pay attention to the details included, and write down your observations and questions. Begin your time with prayer, and, if possible, read the text out loud.

READ 1 SAMUEL 17:1–54

1. Go back through the text and observe:

   a. Who are the main characters in this story? How are they described?

   b. What happens in the story? I've broken it down into four scenes. Briefly (2–3 sentences) summarize each scene in your own words.

   • 17:1–11

   • 17:12–30

   • 17:31–40

   • 17:41–54

c. Who is saved in this story, and by what means are they saved?

2. Describe what Goliath took into battle (vv. 5–7) and what David took into battle (vv. 40, 45).

3. Read verses 8–9. In what ways is this situation different from a typical war between two nations?

4. Read verse 25. What three things will the king do for the man who defeats Goliath?

5. According to verse 34–35, whose sheep did David keep?

   a. Describe how he protected them.

   b. What attacked the sheep?

6. What word does David use twice to describe God (vv. 26, 36)?

7. What does David tell Goliath he is going to do (v. 46)? What does he do (v. 51)?

8. According to verses 52–53, what did the Israelites do?

9. Did any details in the story surprise or confuse you? Do you have any questions about the passage?

The 54 verses we're studying this week contain all the drama of any blockbuster movie. We see family conflict, a cowardly king, a terrifying villain, an unlikely hero, and a victory for the underdog. David was everything we should want a hero to be—courageous, determined, and faithful. He showed his people what a true king is supposed to do. A true king should do battle on behalf of his subjects. A true king should protect his people and stand in their defense. A true king should be willing to lay his life down for his people. David was a true king.

What Does the Text Mean?

Today we'll spend time going deeper in our understanding as we seek to interpret the text. Begin your time with prayer, asking God to give you wisdom and insight as you study.

READ 1 SAMUEL 17:1-54

In yesterday's homework you read that Goliath was wearing a coat of armor weighing approximately 125 pounds. This coat, depending on what translation of the Bible you are using, was called either a "coat of mail" (ESV, NKJV, RSV) or "scale armor" (CSB, NIV, NASB). One commentator said that this armor was "not [like chainmail] made of rings worked together like chains, [but] a coat made of plates of brass lying one upon another like scales."[1] In other words, when Goliath walked out to taunt Israel, he looked like a giant, brass serpent.

1. In light of Genesis 3:15, how significant do you think it is that Goliath was covered in scales? Why?

2. Write down what God promised in Genesis 3:15. What happened to Goliath's head? What was the result for God's people?

---

[1] Carl Friedrich Keil and Franz Delitzsc, *Commentary on the Old Testament: Joshua, Judges, Ruth, 1 and 2 Samuel* (Peabody: Hendrickson Publishers, 1996), 481.

3. In what ways are we like the Israelites?

4. In verse 4, Goliath is called "a champion." Look up the word "champion" and write down the definition that you think best fits. Why do you think Goliath was called a champion?

5. Read 1 Samuel 8:19–20. What did the people expect their king to do for them? If you were an ancient Israelite, encamped in the Valley of Elah, hearing the threats and taunts by this giant of a man for 40 days, how do you think you would feel about the fact that your king, Saul, was not willing to go to battle and defend you?

6. What gave David his courage and confidence (vv. 37, 45, 47)?

7. What do you learn about God in this passage? What do you learn about mankind?

The Israelites did not engage in the epic battle between David and the man who represented the seed of the serpent, Goliath. They cowered in fear, hoping the boy from Bethlehem would defeat their enemy. When he did, the Israelites ran behind their champion, receiving his victory as if it were their own. They received the plunder, the benefits, and the triumph that were rightfully won by another. Because of David's faithfulness and courage, all of God's people were free.

What Does the New Testament Say?

Like we've already said, the story of David and Goliath is probably familiar to most of us. You might have grown up with a flannelgraph depiction of this story in Sunday school. Or, depending on your age, you might have grown up watching cute animated vegetables reenact Bible stories, and you know a few songs about how little people can do big things too. Most of us have heard this story taught under the auspice of learning how we can be like David and fight our giants. Hopefully, you'll see that this story is so much more. Even though there is much to emulate in David, we don't identify with David in the story. We're Israel.

Today we'll spend our time going deeper in our understanding, studying how the New Testament sheds light and gives us fuller meaning. Take time to read the passage again. Begin your time with prayer, asking God to give you wisdom as you study.

READ 1 SAMUEL 17:1–54

1. Read John 10:11–13.

   a. What does Jesus call himself?

   b. What act is required for this to be true?

   c. How does Jesus compare the good shepherd and the hired hand?

d. What is the difference between what David did and what Jesus did?

2. 1 Corinthians 15:22 says, "For as in Adam all die, so also in Christ shall all be made alive." What similarities do you see between this truth and what happened between the Philistines and the Israelites? Describe how your fate is completely wrapped up in the One who represents you.

3. Read Hebrews 2:14–15. How did Jesus win his victory? What does he do for all his people?

4. 1 Corinthians 15:55–57 is one of the greatest declarations of victory in all of Scripture. What is defeated? How? For whom?

5. Read Romans 8:31–39 What benefits of Christ's victory are ours?

The ultimate battle has been fought and won on our behalf. We simply receive the victory and all it means. But that doesn't mean we never face opposition. Scripture is clear that, until Jesus comes again, our defeated enemy still prowls around (1 Pet. 5:8). He cannot have those who belong to Jesus, but he does taunt, tempt, and try us all the same. We are called to fight these battles, not as those who might lose but as those who stand in the victory already won for us.

6. Read Ephesians 6:10–17. Write down each piece of armor we're given and a brief description of how you think each might protect you. How does the story of David and Goliath give you strength, courage, and peace in spiritual battles?

Our entire salvation is wrapped up in our champion. Everyone in Christ is given victory, life, blessing, protection, and eternal salvation. But if you are not in Christ, none of these things is yours. The good news is that if you confess you need a champion and acknowledge Jesus won the battle on your behalf, you become a part of his people and are transferred from death to life (John 5:24). As you work on your memory verse today, thank our living God that he fought and won the battle so we can live.

How Does the Text Transform Me?

READ 1 SAMUEL 17:1–54

As you study this story today, ask the Lord to show how to apply it to your life. In what ways does the story of David and Goliath inform what you believe, how you live, and what you love?

1. As you consider this story, how does it help you better understand your salvation in Christ?

2. What comfort do you find in the phrase, "For the battle is the LORD's" (v. 47)?

3. In what ways do you feel afraid or feel the taunts and threats of the enemy? How can you fight the enemy with the promises of God? What specific promise from God's Word is especially meaningful to you today?

4. How does this story help you rest more in the finished work of Christ?

As we've seen, we live in the time after Jesus came and waged war on our behalf. He has already won the battle. As a result, we stand firm in his victory. We no longer need to fear the enemy because we belong to the One who has already crushed his head.

5. What causes you to tremble with fear like the Israelites in this story? How can you look to God for rescue and confidently entrust your fears to him?

6. Goliath boasted in himself—trusting in his strength and his accomplishments. What areas are you most tempted to boast in when it comes to your abilities? In what ways can you trust in what you're naturally good at instead of leaning on God?

7. David boasted in the Lord. Read 1 Corinthians 1:26–31 and comment on how this helps you boast not in yourself but, rather, in what God has done for you. Write a short prayer telling the Lord the ways you boast in him.

We said on Day 1 that a true king should do battle on behalf of his subjects, protect and defend them, and be willing to lay down his life for his people. David was a true king, but his reign was still marked by sin and failure. Jesus is the greater David, the perfect King, the eternal King of all kings. David risked his life to defeat Israel's enemy, but Jesus actually laid his life down in a brutal death to defeat our ultimate enemies of sin, death, and the ancient serpent (Col. 2:13–15). Then he picked his life up in a decisive victory over those enemies (John 10:17–18). May we rejoice in Christ's victory and rest in his strength.

I'm not a huge sports enthusiast—unless I have a child on the team. I absolutely loved watching my children play sports, especially soccer. I was a rain, shine, snow, sweat kind of fan. I'm a pacing, cheering, yelling kind of soccer mom. When my oldest children started playing, I didn't know much about the game. But I learned it and loved it.

I had a love/hate relationship with those high-stakes games that went into overtime. If you're not a soccer enthusiast, let me explain. If the game is still tied in overtime, the officials will often call for the winner to be determined through a series of penalty kicks. In this scenario, one player goes out by himself or herself and has one chance to score against the opposing team's goalie. The entire fate of the team rests on whether or not the one teammate makes the goal.

When that goal is scored, the player who made the goal is rushed, slapped on the back, congratulated, and celebrated. But the reality is, that one goal wasn't the only thing that won the game. Many moments contributed to a victory—good passes, strong defense, and previous goals. The penalty kick was the high point, but it wasn't the only moment that won the game.

In a similar way, a lot of us understand and explain salvation as "Jesus died on the cross to forgive my sins." This is true—but it's not all. The death and resurrection of Jesus are the definitive high points in our salvation. Those events caused all of creation to hold its breath, wondering if victory would be ours. On the cross Jesus took our sin and crucified it. When Jesus walked out of the tomb, death was defeated. So, yes, his death and resurrection are the decisive, ultimate moments that won our salvation.

But two events preceded the pivotal events above—his incarnation and his perfect, sinless life. Both of these had to occur for his death and resurrection to be effective. And both of these teach us something about what Jesus has done.

We love to talk about the incarnation at Christmas time. Affirming that the eternal Son of God took on flesh and came to earth as a human being is an absolute necessity for our salvation. Galatians 4:4–5 says, "But when the fullness of time had come, God sent forth his Son, born of woman, born under the law, to redeem those who were under the law, so that we might receive adoption as sons."

Jesus came to us as one of us in order to save the likes of us. As a professor of mine liked to say, "It took God to save us; it took a man to save us." He had to become like us in every way in order to do for us what we could not do. As a man, he faced temptations on our behalf, suffered on our behalf, and died on our behalf. Or as the author of Hebrews says, "Therefore he had to be made like his brothers in every respect, so that he might become a merciful and faithful high priest in the service of God, to make propitiation for the sins of the people. For because he himself has suffered when tempted, he is able to help those who are being tempted" (Heb. 2:17–18).

Closely related to the incarnation of Jesus is his perfectly obedient and sinless life. In Genesis 3, the serpent came to Adam and Eve, tempting them to distrust and disobey God. They did. In Matthew 4 we read how the Devil came to Jesus, tempting him to distrust and disobey. He didn't. But it wasn't just in this moment that Jesus perfectly obeyed. He lived an entirely sinless life. This sinless life not only makes his death and resurrection acceptable to God; it is what enables him to give us his perfect righteousness in exchange for our sinful lives.

David went to his brothers on the battlefield. He willingly stepped forward to fight the giant. And he won. As a result, all of Israel reaped the benefits. Our King, at a much greater cost, came to us. He willingly and obediently stood in our place, fought the battle that would have killed us, and then turned to offer us all the glorious benefits of his victory.

Oh sisters, you're not saved because of what you do. You're saved because of what Jesus did. Rest in his completed work. Remember all he has done to save you. And rejoice in your King who is mighty to save.

1. What is one thing you learned about God this week?

2. What is one way you hope to change?

3. In what way does this salvation story remind you of the joy of your salvation in Christ?

Icebreaker Question

What is your favorite epic war movie?

Warm-Up Question

Describe a time when someone defended you
(or you wish they had).

READ 1 SAMUEL 17:1–54

1. Most of us have probably heard of the story of David and Goliath. As you studied this passage this week, did anything new in the story stand out to you as particularly significant?

2. What insights did you gain by seeing Jesus as our greater David?

3. In light of Genesis 3:15, how significant do you think it is that Goliath was covered in scales? Why?

4. What gave David his courage and confidence (vv. 37, 45, 47)?

5. What comfort do you find in the phrase, "For the battle is the LORD's" (v. 47)?

6. What are some practical ways you can allow this story to cultivate great faith and confidence in Christ?

7. What causes you to tremble with fear like the Israelites in this story? How can you look to God for rescue and confidently entrust your fears to him? What specific promise from God's Word is especially meaningful to you today?

8. How were you encouraged or challenged this week?

The King's Table

Salvation Is an Invitation to a Feast

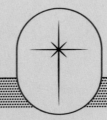

Melissa Kruger

INTRODUCTION

Last week, we studied the story of David and Goliath, rejoicing in the God who rescues. At that point in his life, David was a young shepherd boy, carrying a sling and some stones. In our study this week, he is king of Israel and a victorious warrior many times over. Through David's kindness to Mephibosheth (Meh-FIHB-oh-shehth, what a great name!), we'll have an opportunity to consider the kindness of God. We're rescued from our brokenness, frailty, and sin, and we're welcomed home—to feast at the King's table.

MEMORY VERSE

"And David said to him, 'Do not fear, for I will show you kindness for the sake of your father Jonathan, and I will restore to you all the land of Saul your father, and you shall eat at my table always.'"

2 Samuel 9:7

PRAYER FOR THE WEEK

Father, thank you for these Old Testament stories and how they all point to my greater salvation in Christ. Thank you for seeking me, rescuing me, and giving me life in your name. Open my eyes that I may see the glorious good news of your work in my life. Let me live with hope, joy, peace, and patience as I await your return. Teach me by your Spirit this week. May your Word guide me in all godliness and goodness. Thank you for sending Jesus and for letting me feast at his table.

In Jesus's name I pray. Amen.

What Does the Text Say?

We're going to spend our time today simply observing the text. Good observation begins with listening to the story and absorbing all the details. Begin your time with prayer, and then read the text carefully. If possible, read it out loud.

READ 2 SAMUEL 9:1–13

1. Go back through the text and observe:

   a. Consider the characters in this story. How are they described?

   - David

   - Mephibosheth

   - Ziba

   - Jonathan

b. What happens in the story? Briefly summarize the story in your own words.

c. Who is saved in this story, and by what means are they saved?

2. How does Mephibosheth greet David?

3. What does David say in response (v. 7)?

4. What does David promise Mephibosheth?

5. How does Mephibosheth respond (v. 8)?

6. In what ways does David fulfill his promise?

7. Where did Mephibosheth eat? In what way? For how long?

8. Did any details in the story surprise or confuse you? Do you have any questions about the passage?

142

What Does the Text Mean?

Today we'll spend our time going deeper in our understanding as we seek to interpret the text. Good interpretation flows from thoughtful observation, so take the time to read the passage again. Begin your time with prayer, asking God to give you wisdom as you study.

READ 2 SAMUEL 9:1–13

Saul was Israel's first king. After David killed Goliath, Saul was impressed with David and set him over his men of war (1 Sam. 18:5). But as David's success grew and his fame spread, Saul grew angry and fearful because he knew the Lord was with David (1 Sam. 18:12). On multiple occasions, Saul sought to kill David. However, Jonathan (Saul's son) loved David, made a covenant with him, and protected him (1 Sam. 18:1–4).

1. Read 1 Samuel 20:12–17.

    a. What did Jonathan promise David?

    b. What did Jonathan ask of David (vv. 14–15)?

    c. How did Jonathan feel about David?

2. Consider these passages:

Now Abimelech the son of Jerubbaal went to Shechem to his mother's relatives and said to them and to the whole clan of his mother's family, "Say in the ears of all the leaders of Shechem, 'Which is better for you, that all seventy of the sons of Jerubbaal rule over you, or that one rule over you?' Remember also that I am your bone and your flesh." And his mother's relatives spoke all these words on his behalf in the ears of all the leaders of Shechem, and their hearts inclined to follow Abimelech, for they said, "He is our brother." And they gave him seventy pieces of silver out of the house of Baal-berith with which Abimelech hired worthless and reckless fellows, who followed him. And he went to his father's house at Ophrah and killed his brothers the sons of Jerubbaal, seventy men, on one stone. But Jotham the youngest son of Jerubbaal was left, for he hid himself. And all the leaders of Shechem came together, and all Beth-millo, and they went and made Abimelech king, by the oak of the pillar at Shechem. (Judg. 9:1–6)

Then he wrote to them a second letter, saying, "If you are on my side, and if you are ready to obey me, take the heads of your master's sons and come to me at Jezreel tomorrow at this time." Now the king's sons, seventy persons, were with the great men of the city, who were bringing them up. And as soon as the letter came to them, they took the king's sons and slaughtered them, seventy persons, and put their heads in baskets and sent them to him at Jezreel. . . . So Jehu struck down all who remained of the house of Ahab in Jezreel, all his great men and his close friends and his priests, until he left him none remaining. (2 Kings 10:6–7, 11)

When Jehoram had ascended the throne of his father and was established, he killed all his brothers with the sword, and also some of the princes of Israel. (2 Chron. 21:4)

a. What did these kings do when they came to power?

b. Why do you think they did that?

c. Why do you think Jonathan asked David to protect his life and show kindness to his descendants when he became king?

3. After the death of Saul and Jonathan, we're told, "There was a long war between the house of Saul and the house of David. And David grew stronger and stronger, while the house of Saul became weaker and weaker" (2 Sam. 3:1). As David came to power, all the family of Saul began to flee. Read 2 Samuel 4:1–4. What do you learn about Mephibosheth? How old was he?

4. Considering his background, how do you think Mephibosheth felt when King David sent for him to come to his home? What clues do you get from David's first words to Mephibosheth?

5. What is significant about David's question in 2 Samuel 9:1?

6. Why did David want to show kindness to Mephibosheth?

7. Why is it significant that Mephibosheth ate at David's table like one of his sons?

What Does the New Testament Say?

Today we'll spend our time going deeper in our understanding as we seek to interpret the text by reading a few New Testament passages that help us make gospel connections. Good interpretation flows from thoughtful observation, so take the time to read these passages and consider them in light of David's kindness to Mephibosheth. Begin your time with prayer, asking God to give you wisdom as you study.

READ 2 SAMUEL 9:1–13

For the sake of Jonathan, Mephibosheth was welcomed into King David's home, given a seat at his table, and treated like a son. Today, we'll consider how in a similar way, we are invited to our King's table and treated as his beloved children.

1. Read Galatians 4:1–7.

    a. What did Jesus redeem us from?

    b. What are we adopted into?

2. Read Romans 5:6–10. What four words are used to describe what we were like before we became Christians? In what ways are these words similar to how David may have viewed Mephibosheth?

3. Read 1 John 2:12. For whose sake does God forgive us? How is this similar to why David looked with favor on Mephibosheth?

4. David welcomed Mephibosheth to his table to eat as one of his sons. Read the following passages and write out what table we are invited to as members of God's family.

   a. Luke 22:14–20

   b. Revelation 19:9

   c. Revelation 22:17 (see also Isa. 55:1–3)

   d. Why do we get to eat these meals?

5. David not only invited Mephibosheth to eat at his table, he gave him a home, land, and provision. Read John 14:1–7. In what ways does God promise to provide for his children?

6. Throughout this study we've traced the promised seed from Genesis. We've seen God keep his promise as he protected the offspring of Abraham. In this story, we also get a glimpse of how the promised offspring will live and act. Read 1 John 3:1–10 and fill out the chart below, comparing the actions of the children of God and the children of the Devil.

Children of the Devil	Children of God
Makes a practice of sinning	Hopes in God, purifies himself

7. As you consider this passage, how can we recognize a child of God? How do they live? At what table do they eat? Where is their true home?

How Does the Text Transform Me?

We've observed the text and interpreted its meaning. Now it's time to take what we've studied and apply it to our lives. Pray for the Spirit to transform you as you study God's Word today.

READ 2 SAMUEL 9:1–13

1. In this story, David didn't wait until Mephibosheth came knocking on his door, asking for help. In remembrance of Jonathan's kindness, David initiated and pursued Mephibosheth with kindness. Take some time to consider the people in your life. Who can you actively pursue with kindness as you remember God's kindness to you? How can you do that today? This week? This month?

2. 1 Thessalonians 5:14–15 instructs, "And we urge you, brothers, admonish the idle, encourage the fainthearted, help the weak, be patient with them all. See that no one repays anyone evil for evil, but always seek to do good to one another and to everyone."

    a. How was David an example of this verse?

    b. Is there someone in your life who you are tempted to "repay evil for evil"? As you consider Christ's kindness to you, in what ways could you treat that person with kindness?

3. Is it difficult for you to believe you are a child of God? Why or why not? In what ways do you wrongly try to "earn" your adoption? Instead, how does the story of David and Mephibosheth help you rest and rejoice in your adoption?

4. Read Ephesians 2:11–22. Why do you think Paul wanted them to remember what they used to be? How would remembering their past give them present joy? Thinking about the story we studied this week, take a few minutes to write out what your life used to look like apart from Christ. Then write out what Jesus has done in your life, thanking him for rescuing you and bringing you into his kingdom.

5. Yesterday, we read 1 John 3:1–10. Are there any areas of your life where you are "making a practice of sinning" (living in opposition to God's Word and being unwilling to stop)? Spend some time praying and asking God if there are any areas in your life that you need to repent of in order to walk in newness of life. If you feel hard-hearted toward God and unwilling to repent, tell him that and ask him to soften your heart. Be encouraged—Jesus appeared to destroy the works of the Devil (v. 8). He can answer your prayer and give you freedom to walk in righteousness.

6. When David allowed Mephibosheth to sit at his table, it meant more than just a free meal. It meant Mephibosheth had access to the king and to information about the kingdom. In what ways do you have a similar access to God through Christ? Are you taking advantage of his invitation to talk to him through prayer and listen to him through his Word? Why or why not?

7. As you consider this story, how does it help you better understand your salvation in Christ? How does David's kindness to Mephibosheth foreshadow God's kindness to you?

8. Jesus is preparing a heavenly home for you. Isn't that amazing? How does that future hope encourage you to view your current home and possessions differently? In what ways can you live in greater freedom with regard to earthly treasures as you consider your heavenly inheritance?

9. As you consider the story this week, how does David's kindness to Mephibosheth encourage you to believe, live, or love differently?

A few weeks ago, a friend invited me over for dinner. When I asked what I could bring, she replied, "Just bring yourself." When I got to her house, I was overwhelmed by her kindness. There were appetizers, delicious food, and multiple options for dessert. We spent hours chatting as we enjoyed the meal together.

Typically, it's a kindness to be invited to someone's home. However, for Mephibosheth, it was most likely a fearful thing to be summoned to the king's palace. As a descendant of King Saul, he was a potential rival for Israel's throne.

Mephibosheth was only 5 years old when his father died, and the resulting turmoil left him lame in both feet. Mostly likely, he couldn't remember his father very well and wouldn't have known about the covenant friendship between his father and David. In Mephibosheth's mind, he was fatherless, crippled, and an enemy of the king. Why would David be inviting him? Surely it was to finish off all the remaining heirs of Saul so that David could secure his throne from any final threats or opponents.

Instead of violence, David immediately put him at ease and met Mephibosheth with kindness: "Do not fear, for I will show you kindness for the sake of your father Jonathan, and I will restore to you all the land of Saul your father, and you shall eat at my table always" (2 Sam. 9:7).

Notice that David didn't have dinner with Mephibosheth first. He didn't try to figure out if Mephibosheth was a threat or if he was favorable to David's kingship. He immediately showed him warmth and kindness because of his love for Jonathan. He bestowed property, servants, and sonship to Mephibosheth because of the covenant he made with Jonathan.

Mephibosheth came to the palace poor, fatherless, and an enemy of the king—he considered himself "a dead dog" (2 Sam. 9:8). He left that day a wealthy man, invited to feast at the king's table, welcomed like one of David's own sons. All of this was given to him for the sake of Jonathan.

It's a beautiful picture of a life radically changed because of grace. It's my story, and it's yours too. It's the story of every person who has accepted the gracious invitation of God:

> Come, everyone who thirsts,
> come to the waters;
> and he who has no money,
> come, buy and eat!
> Come, buy wine and milk
> without money and without price.
> Why do you spend your money for that which is not bread,
> and your labor for that which does not satisfy?
> Listen diligently to me, and eat what is good,
> and delight yourselves in rich food.
> Incline your ear, and come to me;
> hear, that your soul may live;
> and I will make with you an everlasting covenant,
> my steadfast, sure love for David. (Isa. 55:1–3)

How can God offer such an invitation? We are weak, ungodly, crippled because of sin, and enemies of God (Rom. 5:6–10). And yet, he invites us to a soul-satisfying feast. Why?

For the sake of Jesus.

Peter tells us, "For Christ also suffered once for sins, the righteous for the unrighteous, that he might bring us to God" (1 Pet. 3:18). Jesus paid the bloody price so that we might freely come to God and enjoy all the benefits of feasting at his table. Currently, the church shares a meal—communion—to remember his body that was broken for us and his blood that was poured out for us (1 Cor. 11: 23–26). It's a foretaste of an even better meal that's coming when we will eat together at the wedding feast of the Lamb (Rev. 19:9.) And we don't bring anything to this feast—just ourselves.

How do we live as we wait for that day? Romans 5:10–11 tells us: "For if while we were enemies we were reconciled to God by the death of his Son, much more, now that we are reconciled, shall we be saved by his life. More than that, we also rejoice in God through our Lord Jesus Christ, through whom we have now received reconciliation." As God's people, we walk in newness of life, rejoicing that we have received reconciliation. As we have received kindness and mercy, we extend it to others.

As you've studied these stories of salvation over the past seven lessons, I hope they've renewed your joy. If you doubt that you're good enough to be at God's table, look back at the work of Jesus. He lived a perfect life, and he paid the price so you can feast. If you're weary of this world and desperate for something better, look forward to an eternity with Jesus (with no more tears, death, or pain). His past work and future promises supply our present joy. The promised offspring of the woman has crushed the head of the serpent so you can come and dine with the King of kings. Rest in him today, rejoicing that you've been invited to the feast:

"Behold, I stand at the door and knock. If anyone hears my voice and opens the door, I will come in to him and eat with him, and he with me" (Rev. 3:20).

1. What is one thing you learned about God this week?

2. What is one way you hope to change?

3. In what way does this salvation story remind you of the joy of your salvation in Christ?

Icebreaker Question

What's your favorite meal to serve when having people over for dinner?

Warm-Up Question

Can you share of a time when enjoying a meal with someone at their home made you feel like a part of their family? What did they do that made you feel so welcome?

READ 2 SAMUEL 9:1–13

1. In what ways did David show kindness to Mephibosheth?

2. Why was David's kindness to Mephibosheth surprising? Why did he show him kindness?

3. Read Romans 5:6–10. What four words are used to describe what we were like before we became Christians? Why is it surprising that God showed us kindness? How is God's kindness similar to David's? In what ways is it even greater?

4. Why is it such good news that God's kindness to us is for the sake of Christ and not our own merits or righteousness? In what ways

does that allow you to freely and boldly approach his throne (see Heb. 4:16)?

5. When David allowed Mephibosheth to sit at his table, it meant more than just a free meal. It meant Mephibosheth had access to the king and to information about the kingdom. In what ways do we have similar access to God through Christ?

6. Jesus is preparing a heavenly home for you. How does that future hope encourage you to view your current home and possessions differently? In what ways can you live with greater freedom with regard to earthly treasures as you consider your heavenly inheritance?

7. Share with your group how this salvation story reminds you of the joy of your salvation in Christ.

8. Spend some time reviewing the stories you've studied these past seven weeks. Which story affected you the most? How did these stories help grow your understanding of the Bible and your salvation in Christ? In what ways have these stories restored the joy of your salvation?

About TGC

The Gospel Coalition (TGC) supports the church in making disciples of all nations, by providing gospel-centered resources that are trusted and timely, winsome and wise.

Guided by a Council of more than 40 pastors in the Reformed tradition, TGC seeks to advance gospel-centered ministry for the next generation by producing content (including articles, podcasts, videos, courses, and books) and convening leaders (including conferences, virtual events, training, and regional chapters).

In all of this we want to help Christians around the world better grasp the gospel of Jesus Christ and apply it to all of life in the 21st century. We want to offer biblical truth in an era of great confusion. We want to offer gospel-centered hope for the searching.

Join us by visiting TGC.org so you can be equipped to love God with all your heart, soul, mind, and strength, and to love your neighbor as yourself.